Pentecostal Truth

TWELVE LESSONS
(DIVIDED IN TWO UNITS)

by

Myer Pearlman and Frank M. Boyd

Address all communications to—
BEREAN SCHOOL OF THE BIBLE
(CORRESPONDENCE SCHOOL OF THE ASSEMBLIES OF GOD)
1445 BOONVILLE AVENUE • SPRINGFIELD, MISSOURI 65802

[PRINTED
IN U·S·A]

Contents

Introduction

At the turn of this century members of various denominations became concerned about the spiritual condition of the church and the world. As a result they began earnestly to seek the Lord for a spiritual renewal. It was not long before believers were having experiences like those described in the Book of Acts. In most cases, the established churches repudiated these experiences and frequently by request, the Spirit-filled believers found it necessary to leave the churches with which they had been affiliated. As these believers of many denominations were drawn together by their common experiences they came to be known as "The Pentecostal Movement" or "Tongues People."

But what do we mean by "the Pentecostal Movement" or "the Tongues People"? Is it that we exist simply to magnify "tongues" as such? Certainly not. Is it even that we desire primarily to magnify one experience of the Christian life, the baptism in the Spirit, above the totality of the gracious dynamic and sanctifying operations of the third Person of the Trinity? No, not even this.

The answer is that we are Pentecostal because we desire to honor the personal Holy Spirit who came dispensationally on the Day of Pentecost, the divine Administrator in the church during this present age, in *all* the fullness of His workings in convicting, baptizing, filling, sanctifying, guiding, and above all in

5

His purpose to make our Lord Jesus Christ a living reality in the daily walk of the believer (John 14: 16-18; 16:13, 14).

The doctrine of the Holy Spirit, judged by the place it occupies in the Scriptures, stands in the foremost rank of redemption truths. With the exception of 2 and 3 John, every book in the New Testament contains a reference to the Spirit's work; every Gospel begins with a promise of His outpouring.

Yet it is admittedly the "neglected doctrine." Formalism and fear of fanaticism have produced a reaction against emphasis on the Spirit's work in personal experience.

Naturally this has resulted in spiritual deadness, for there can be no vital Christianity apart from the Spirit. Only He can make actual what Christ's work has made possible. In the words of Ignatius, a leader of the ancient church:

"The grace of the Spirit brings the machinery of redemption into vital connection with the individual soul. Apart from the Spirit the Cross stands inert, a vast machine at rest, and about it lie the stones of the building unmoved. Not till the rope has been attached can the work proceed of lifting the individual life through faith and love to the place prepared for it in the church of God."

UNIT ONE

Lessons 1 to 8

Lesson 1

NAMES OF THE HOLY SPIRIT

Who is the Holy Spirit? The answer to this question will be found in studying the names He bears, and the symbols which illustrate His workings.

a. The Spirit of God. The Spirit is the executive of the Godhead—working in every sphere, both physical and moral. Through the Spirit, God created and preserves the universe. Through the Spirit—"the finger of God" (Luke 11:20) —God works in the spiritual sphere, converting sinners and sanctifying and sustaining believers.

(1) Is the Holy Spirit divine in the absolute sense? His deity is proved from the following facts: Divine attributes are ascribed to Him; He is eternal, omnipresent, omnipotent, and omniscient (Hebrews 9:14; Psalm 139:7-10; Luke 1:35; 1 Corinthians 2:10, 11). Divine works are ascribed to Him such as creation, regeneration and resurrection (Genesis 1:2; Job 33:4; John 3:5-8; Romans 8:11). He is placed in coordinate rank with the Father and the Son (1 Corinthians 12: 4-6; 2 Corinthians 13:14; Matthew 28:19; Revelation 1:4).

(2) Is the Holy Spirit a person or just an influence? The Spirit is often described in an impersonal way—

as the Breath that fills, the Unction that anoints, the
Fire that lights and heats, the Water that is poured
out, the Gift of which all may partake. However, these
are merely descriptions of His operations. The Spirit
is described in such a way as to leave no doubt as to
His personality. (a) He exercises the attributes of personality: mind (Romans 8:27), will (1 Corinthians
12:11), feeling (Ephesians 4:30). (b) Personal activities are ascribed to Him: He reveals (2 Peter 1:21),
teaches (John 14:26), witnesses (Galatians 4:6), in-
tercedes (Romans 8:26), speaks (Revelation 2:7), com-
mands (Acts 16:6, 7), testifies (John 15:26). (c) At-
titudes are assumed toward Him which could be exhibited only toward personality: He may be grieved
(Ephesians 4:30), lied to (Acts 5:3), and blasphemed
(Matthew 12:31, 32). (d) His personality is indicated
by the fact that He is distinguished from His gifts
(1 Corinthians 12:11).

Perhaps some have denied personality to the Spirit
because He is not described as having body or shape.
But personality and corporeality (possessing a body)
must be distinguished. Personality is that which pos-
sesses intelligence, feeling, and will; it does not necessarily require a body. Moreover, lack of definite form
is no argument against reality. The wind is real though
without form (John 3:8).

It is not difficult to form a conception of God the
Father or of the Lord Jesus Christ, but some have con-
fessed to an inability to form a clear conception of
the Holy Spirit. The reason is twofold: First, throughout the Scriptures the Spirit's operations are invisible,
secret, and internal. Second, the Holy Spirit never

speaks of Himself or represents Himself; He always comes in the name of and as representing another. He is hidden behind the Lord Jesus Christ and in the depths of our inner man. He never calls attention to Himself but to the will of God and the saving work of Christ. "He shall not speak of himself," i.e., as from a separate store of knowledge (John 16:13).

(3) Is the Holy Spirit a personality distinct from God the Father? Yes; the Spirit proceeds from God, is sent from God, is God's gift to men.

In fact, He is God in His ability to extend Himself to the infinite reaches of limitless space. Cf. Psalm 139.

Yet the Spirit is not independent of God. He always represents the one God acting in the spheres of thought, will and activity. How the Spirit can be one with God and yet distinct from God is part of the mystery of the Trinity.

Lesson 2

NAMES OF THE HOLY SPIRIT (Continued)

b. The Spirit of Christ (Romans 8:9). There is no essential distinction between the Spirit of God, the Spirit of Christ, and the Holy Spirit. For there is only one Holy Spirit, as there can be only one God and one Son. But the one Spirit has many names descriptive of His various ministries.

Why is the Spirit called the Spirit of Christ? (1) Because He is sent in the name of Christ (John 14: 26). (2) Because He is the Spirit sent by the Christ. The Spirit is the principle of spiritual life by which men are born into the kingdom of God. This new life of the Spirit is imparted and maintained by Christ (John 1:12, 13; 4:10; 7:38), who is also the baptizer with the Holy Spirit (Matthew 3:11). (3) The Holy Spirit is called the Spirit of Christ because His special mission in this age is to glorify Christ (John 16:14). His special work is connected with Him who lived, died, rose, and ascended. He makes real *in* believers what Christ has done *for* them. (4) The glorified Christ is present in the church and in believers by the Holy Spirit. It is often said that the Spirit has come to take the place of Christ, but it is more correct to say that He has come to make Christ real. The Holy Spirit makes possible and real the omnipresence of Christ in the world (Matthew 18:20) and His indwelling in believers. The connection between Christ and the Spirit is so close that both Christ and the Spirit are said to dwell in the believer (Galatians 2:20; Romans 8:9, 10) ; and the believer is both "in Christ" and "in the Spirit."

Thanks to the Holy Spirit, the life of Christ becomes our life in Christ.

c. The Comforter. This is the title given to the Spirit in John, chapters 14-17. A study of the background of these chapters will reveal the significance of the gift. The disciples had taken their last meal with the Master. Their hearts were sad at the thought of His departure, and they were oppressed with a sense of weakness and helplessness. Who will help us when He is gone? Who will teach and guide us? Who will stand by us as we preach and teach? How shall we be able to face a hostile world? These unspoken fears Jesus quieted with the promise, "I will pray the Father, and he shall give you *another* Comforter, that he may abide with you for ever" (John 14:16).

The word Comforter, "paracletos" in the Greek, bears the following literal meaning: one called to the side of another for the purpose of helping him in any way, particularly in legal proceedings; a succorer. It was the custom in ancient tribunals for parties to appear in court attended by one or more of their most influential friends, who were called in Greek, "paracletes," and in Latin, "advocates." These gave their friends—not for fee or reward, but from love and interest—the advantage of their personal presence and

the aid of their wise counsel. They advised them what
to do and what to say, spoke for them, acted on their
behalf, made the cause of their friends their own
cause, stood by them and for them in the trials, difficulties, and dangers of the situation.

Such was the relationship that the Lord Jesus had
sustained to the disciples during His earthly ministry,
and naturally they were dismayed at the thought of
His departure. But He comforted them with the promise of another Comforter who should be their defender,
helper, and teacher during His absence. He is called
"another" Comforter because He was to be invisibly
to the disciples what Jesus had been to them visibly.

The word "another" distinguishes the Holy Spirit
from Jesus, yet puts Him on the same plane. Jesus
sends the Spirit, yet Jesus comes spiritually to the disciples through the Spirit; the Spirit is thus both
Christ's Successor and also His Presence. The Holy
Spirit makes possible and real the continued presence
of Christ in the church.

"It is He who causes the person of Christ to dwell
in them so that they acquire the right to say with Paul,
'Christ liveth in me.' It is therefore the life of Christ,
the nature of Christ, the sentiments of Christ, the virtues of Christ, that the Spirit communicates to believers; it is after the likeness of Christ that He fashions
them, and after the model which He had left us. Without Christ the Spirit has nothing to produce in the
heart of the believer. Take away Christ and His Word,
and it is like removing from the photographer's studio
the person whose features the sun is about to fix on
the plate prepared to receive them.

The sending of the Comforter does not mean that Christ has ceased to be the Helper and Advocate of His people. John tells us that He still fulfills that office (1 John 2:1). Christ, whose sphere of work is in heaven, defends the disciples against the charges of the "accuser of the brethren"; at the same time the Spirit, whose sphere of work is on earth, "silences the earthly adversaries of the Church through the victory of faith which overcomes the world." As Christ is Paraclete in heaven, so the Holy Ghost is Paraclete on earth.

The ascended Christ not only sends the Spirit but also manifests Himself by means of the Spirit. In the flesh He could be in only one place at a time; in His ascended life He is omnipresent by the Spirit. During His earthly life He was external to men; by the Spirit He can dwell in the very depths of their souls. One writer has stated this truth as follows:

"If He had remained on earth in His physical life, He would have been only an example to be copied; but if He went to His Father and sent His Spirit, then He would be a life to be lived. If he had remained visibly and tangibly with us, He would have been related to us merely as a model is related to an artist who chisels his marble, but never as the idea and inspiration which produces the work of art. If He had remained on earth, He would have been merely the subject of prolonged observation of scientific study, and He would always have been outside of us, external to us; an external voice, an external life, an external example.... But thanks to His Spirit, He can now live in us as the very Soul of our souls, the very Spirit of our spirits, the Truth of our minds, the Love of our hearts, and the Desire of our wills."

If the Spirit's work is to communicate the work of the Son, what gain could there be in the departing of the one in order to make possible the coming of the other? *Answer*: It is not the *earthly* Christ that the Spirit communicates, but the *heavenly* Christ—the Christ reinvested with His eternal power, reclothed with heavenly glory. The following is an illustration suggested by Dr. A. J. Gordon:

"It is as if a father, whose kinsman had died, had said to his children: 'We are poor and I have become an heir. If you will submit cheerfully to my leaving you and my crossing the sea and entering into my inheritance, I will send you back a thousand times more than you could have had by my remaining with you.' "

Christ's life on earth represented the days of His poverty (2 Corinthians 8:9) and humiliation; on the Cross He secured the riches of His grace (Ephesians 1:7); on the Throne He secured the riches of His glory (Ephesians 3:16). After His ascension to the Father He sent the Spirit to convey the riches of the inheritance. By His ascension Christ would have more to give and the church would have more to receive (John 16:12; 14:12). "The stream of life will have higher power because of the higher source from which it proceeds."

The Comforter teaches only the things of Christ, yet teaches more than Christ taught. Until the Crucifixion, Resurrection, and Ascension the Christian doctrine was not yet complete and therefore could not be fully communicated to the disciples of Christ. In John 16:

12, 13 Jesus says in effect: "I have brought you a little way in the knowledge of my doctrine; He shall bring you all the way." The Ascension was to bring a larger impartation of *truth* as well as a greater impartation of *power*.

d. The Holy Spirit. The Spirit is called holy because He is the Spirit of the Holy One, and because His chief work is sanctification. We need a Saviour for two reasons: to do something *for* us and something *in* us. Jesus did the first by dying for us. Through the Holy Spirit He does the second; He lives in us, transmitting to our souls His divine life. The Holy Spirit has come to reorganize the nature of man and to pit Himself against all its evil tendencies.

e. The Holy Spirit of Promise. The Holy Spirit is so called because His grace and power is one of the outstanding blessings promised in the Old Testament (Ezekiel 36:27; Joel 2:28). It is the highest prerogative of the Christ, or the Messiah, to impart the Spirit, and this Jesus claimed when He said, "Behold, I send the promise of my Father upon you" (Luke 24:49; Galatians 3:14).

f. The Spirit of Truth. The purpose of the Incarnation was to reveal the Father; the mission of the Comforter is to reveal the *Son.* When we gaze upon a picture, we may for ourselves see much that is beautiful and attractive in its modes of exhibiting color and form; but to understand the inner meaning of the picture and appreciate its real purpose we need some skilled interpreter to open our eyes.

The Holy Spirit is the Interpreter of Jesus Christ.

He does not bestow a new or different revelation, but rather opens the minds of men to see the deeper meaning of Christ's life and words. As the Son did not speak of Himself, but spoke what He received from the Father, so the Spirit will not speak of Himself as from a separate store of knowledge, but will declare what He hears in that inner life of the Godhead.

g. The Spirit of Grace (Hebrews 10:29; Zechariah 12:10). The Holy Spirit gives man grace to repent by striving with him; He imparts the power for sanctification, endurance, and service. He who does despite unto the Spirit of grace drives away Him who alone can touch or move the heart, and thus cuts himself off from God's mercy.

h. The Spirit of Life (Romans 8:2; Revelation 11:11). "I believe in the Holy Ghost, the Lord, and Giver of life," reads an ancient creed. The Spirit is that Person of the Godhead whose special function is the creation and preservation of natural and spiritual life.

i. The Spirit of Adoption (Romans 8:15). When a person is saved, he is not only given the name of "child of God" and adopted into the divine family, but he also receives within his soul the consciousness that he is a partaker of the divine nature. Writes Bishop Andrews: "As Christ is our witness in heaven, so is the Spirit here on earth witnessing with our spirits that we are the children of God."

Lesson 3

THE TRINITY

It might be helpful to introduce at this point a brief discussion of the doctrine of the Trinity or the Triune God, which may enable us more clearly to comprehend the relations of the Holy Spirit to the Father and to the Son, and to understand better various scriptures concerning the Spirit Himself.

The doctrine of the Trinity is not so much declared as intimated in the Old Testament. The main message of the Old Testament is the *unity* of God as revealed to Israel (Deuteronomy 6:4), in contrast with the polytheism of the nations which surrounded them (Isaiah 43:10, 11; 45:5, 6; Deuteronomy 4:35).

This unity is a compound one. Cf. Genesis 1:26— "Let *us* make man in *our* image." Cf. also 3:22. That this image is not angelic and that this apparent council over man's creation was in the circle of the Godhead, is seen in 1:27—"So *God* created man in *his* own image, in the image of God created he him...."

The word used for "God" in these early records of Genesis is *Elohim,* a plural noun; in fact, wherever one finds the ending "im" in Hebrew nouns, the words are plural in meaning.

In the Old Testament we find a series of personal divine manifestations, called theophanies, especially "the angel of the Lord" or "the angel of his presence" (literally—face). Cf. Genesis 18:22; 22:15; 32:

24-32; Judges 6:20-24; Judges 13. "The angel of his presence [face] saved them" (Isaiah 63:9). Who was this angel? We believe the answer is found in 1 Corinthians 10:4—Christ. The word "angel" means simply a messenger or envoy, and can have a proper application to Christ as coming from the "face" or presence of God.

The presence of the Holy Spirit and His active operation are seen in such passages as Genesis 1:2; Judges 6:34; Isaiah 63:10.

The doctrine of the Trinity is clearly taught in the New Testament. It is not merely intimated, as in the Old Testament, but directly declared.

At the baptism of Christ (Matthew 3:16, 17) the Father speaks from the open heavens; the Son is being baptized in the Jordan by John the Baptist; and the Spirit descends upon Christ in the form of a dove.

It is seen in the baptismal formula—"Baptizing them in [or into] the name [singular] of the Father, and of the Son, and of the Holy Ghost" (Matthew 28:19). The conjunction in one name of the Three affirms equality and oneness of substance or essence.

It is shown also in the apostolic benediction—"The grace of our Lord Jesus Christ, . . . love of God, . . . communion of the Holy Ghost" (2 Corinthians 13:14).

Christ Himself taught the doctrine of the Trinity in John 14:16: "*I* will pray the *Father* . . . he will give you *another Comforter.*"

The New Testament sets forth:
A Father who is God (Romans 1:7).
A Son who is God (Hebrews 1:8).
A Holy Spirit who is God (Acts 5:3, 4).

The whole is summed up in the words of Board-man: "The Father is the *fullness* of the Godhead *invisible,* John 1:18; the Son is the *fullness* of the Godhead *manifested,* John 1:14-18; the Spirit is all the *fullness* of the Godhead *acting immediately upon the creature,* 1 Corinthians 2:9, 10. (From *Great Doctrines of the Bible*—Evans.)

In contemplation of this great scriptural doctrine we are faced with mystery too profound for our finite minds to comprehend. It is difficult, if not impossible, aptly to illustrate such mysteries. But there are symbolisms which, when analyzed as far as we can go, help us to grasp in measure this great truth.

As one illustration let us note the *equilateral triangle,* one composed of three equal sides, which subtend three equal angles; in other words, each side of the three is the same in length and each angle is of the same number of degrees—three equal sides, three equal angles, yet *one* triangle.

Formula—Each angle, when extended to the limit of the third side, embraces or takes in the whole triangular area. The three angles all merge into a unity, one triangle, so that we have THREE IN ONE, ONE IN THREE, a tri-unity.

For the sake of comparison, mark one angle the Father, another, the Son, the third, the Holy Spirit, thus:

You will note by using the above formula that each person of the Godhead is all-comprehensive and embraces and includes the other two, THREE IN ONE, ONE IN THREE.

Another symbol is found in LIGHT—"God is light." Physicists have analyzed light as having three component elements or properties:

(1) The *actinic.*

This is the chemico-active property of light or of radiant energy by which chemical changes are produced, as upon the photographic plate, where there is a sensitive emulsion.

This actinic property can *neither* be *seen* nor *felt,* and corresponds to the *Father,* of whom this is true. Cf. 1 Timothy 1:17; 6:16.

(2) The *luminiferous.*

This is the property of light which brings it into manifestation. Here are the phenomena of illumination and warmth.

It can be *both seen* and *felt,* and is the *revealer* of the other two. It corresponds to the *Son of God,* who is the Revealer of the Godhead. Cf. Hebrews 1: 3—"the brightness [forthshining or effulgence] of his glory, the express image [visible representation] of his person"; Colossians 1:15—"the image [likeness] of the invisible God"; John 14:9—"He that hath seen me hath seen the Father."

(3) The *calorific.*

This is the property of light which produces heat. It can be *felt,* but *not seen,* and corresponds to the *Holy Spirit,* who is invisible, yet who manifests the divine presence through energy, which can be felt.

These three properties of light are inseparable; where one is, the others always are present. Light could have no being or existence without all three. Where the actinic is, there are the luminiferous and the calorific; where the luminiferous is, there are the actinic and the calorific; where the calorific is, there are the actinic and the luminiferous. Each is light and there is no light, nor can there be light, where one is absent. In fact, light cannot be conceived of apart from all three properties. It would not be light.

So, as in the illustration of the triangle, where the Father is, there are the Son and the Spirit; where the Son is, there are the Father and the Spirit; where the Spirit is, there are the Father and the Son. Cf. Colossians 1:2, 3; 1 Peter 1:1-3; Ephesians 2:18; 2 Corinthians 13:14.

It seems reasonable and necessary that in the Godhead there should be ONE equal to the Father, with whom, in equal infinite capacity, the Father can share

His glory, whose fellowship He can enjoy, and whose
love the Father can receive and reciprocate. Otherwise
God would be the most isolated, lonely Being in His
whole universe. Since He has made us, His creatures,
with capacity for fellowship with others of like nature,
His infinite Being could be satisfied only in an infinite co-eternal Son.

Then, too, there must be the personal spiritual mode
of manifesting His presence and of contacting the out-
most reaches of His vast universe, for God is not only
transcendent in creation, but immanent as well. "God
is spirit" and through the personal Holy Spirit, the
third person of the Trinity, He can be and is omnipresent.

Lesson 4

SYMBOLS OF THE HOLY SPIRIT

It has been well said that "words are often but lame vehicles for the conveyance of truth. At their best they but half reveal, half conceal the hidden depths of thought." God has chosen to illustrate with symbol what otherwise, because of the poverty of language, we never could know. The following symbols are employed to describe the operations of the Holy Spirit:

a. Fire (Isaiah 4:4; Matthew 3:11; Luke 3:16). Fire illustrates the purging, purification, fiery boldness, and zeal produced by the anointing of the Spirit. The Spirit is compared to fire because fire warms, illuminates, spreads and purifies. Compare Jeremiah 20:9.

b. Wind (Ezekiel 37:7-10; John 3:8; Acts 2:2). Wind symbolizes the regenerative work of the Spirit and is indicative of His mysterious, independent, penetrating, life-giving and purifying operation.

c. Water (Exodus 17:6; Ezekiel 36:25-27; 47:1; John 3:5; 4:14; 7:38, 39). The Spirit is the fountain of living water, the purest, the best, because He is a veritable river of life—flooding, gushing over our souls, cleansing away the dust of sin. The power of the Spirit does in the spiritual what water does in the material order. Water purifies, refreshes, quenches thirst and makes fruitfulness possible. It purifies what is soiled and restores cleanliness; it is an apt symbol of divine grace which not only cleanses the soul but

adds to it a divine beauty. Water is an indispensable
element of physical life; the Holy Spirit is an indispensable element of spiritual life.

What is the meaning of the expression, "living water"? It is living in contrast with the stagnant water
of cisterns or marshes; it is water that bubbles up,
flows along always in communication with its source
and always bearing evidences of life. If this water is
caught in a reservoir, if its flow is interrupted, if it
is cut off from its source, it can no longer bear the
name of living water. Christians have the "living water" only to the extent that they are in contact with
its divine source in Christ.

d. A Seal (Ephesians 1:13; 2 Timothy 2:19). This
illustration conveys the following thoughts: (1) Ownership. The impress of a seal implies a relation to the
owner of the seal, and is a sure token of something
belonging to him. Believers are God's property and
known to be so by the Spirit dwelling in them. The
following custom was common in Ephesus in Paul's
day. A merchant would go to the harbor, select certain
timber and then stamp it with his seal—an acknowl-
edged sign of ownership. Later he would send his
servant with his signet who looked for the timber bearing the corresponding impress. See 2 Timothy 2:19.
(2) The idea of security is also involved. See Ephesians 1:13; compare Revelation 7:3. The Spirit inspires
the sense of security and assurance in the believer's
heart (Romans 8:16). He is an earnest or down pay-
ment of our heavenly inheritance, an assurance of the
glory to come. Christians have been sealed, but must

beware of doing anything to break the seal, i.e., to grieve the Spirit by whom they are sealed (Ephesians 4:30).

e. Oil. Oil is perhaps the most familiar and common symbol of the Spirit. Whenever oil was used ritually in the Old Testament it spoke of usefulness, fruitfulness, beauty, life, and transformation. It was commonly used for food, light, lubrication, healing, and soothing of the skin. In like manner, in the spiritual order the Spirit strengthens, illumines, liberates, heals and soothes the soul.

f. The Dove. The dove, as a symbol, speaks of gentleness, tenderness, loveliness, innocence, mildness, peace, purity, and patience. Among the Syrians it is an emblem of the life-giving powers of nature. A Jewish tradition translates Genesis 1:2 as follows: "The Spirit of God like a dove brooded over the waters." Christ spoke of the dove as the embodiment of the harmlessness which was characteristic of His own disciples.

THE HOLY SPIRIT IN THE OLD TESTAMENT

The Holy Spirit is revealed in the Old Testament in three ways: first, as the creative or cosmic Spirit, through whose power the universe and all living creatures were created; second, as the dynamic or power-giving Spirit; third, as the regenerative Spirit by which human nature is changed.

a. The Creative Spirit

The Holy Spirit is the Third Person of the Trinity by whose power the universe was created. He brooded

over the face of the waters and shared the glory of
creation (Genesis 1:2; Job 26:13; Psalm 33:6; 104:
30). Writes D. Denio:

"The Holy Spirit as Deity immanent (abiding) in all
creation manifests His presence by what we call the
laws of nature. He is the principle of order and life,
the organizing power in created nature. All the forces
of nature are but evidences of the presence and operation of the Spirit of God. Mechanical forces, chemical
action, organic life in plant and animal, energy connected with nervous action, intelligence, and moral
conduct are but tokens of the immanence of God of
which the Holy Spirit is the agent."

The Holy Spirit created and sustains man (Genesis
2:7; Job 33:4). Every individual, whether or not he
serves God, is sustained by the creative power of God's
Spirit (Daniel 5:23; Acts 17:28). Man's existence is
like the note of an organ, lasting only as long as the
Creator's finger is upon the key. Man owes his being
to the "two hands of God," the Word (John 1:1-3) and
the Spirit, for it was to these that the words, "Let
us make man," were spoken.

b. *The Dynamic Spirit*

The Creator-Spirit made man in order that he might
form a society governed by God; in other words, the
kingdom of God. After sin had entered and human
society was organized apart from and in opposition to
God, God made a new start by calling Israel, organizing them under His laws, and so constituting them
the kingdom of Jehovah (2 Chronicles 13:8). As we
study the history of Israel we read of the Holy Spirit

inspiring certain individuals to rule and guide the members of that kingdom and to supervise their progress in the life of consecration.

The dynamic operation of the Spirit created two kinds of ministers: first, workers for God—men of action, organizers, executives; second, speakers for God —prophets and teachers.

(1) *Workers for God.* As examples of Spirit-inspired workers we mention Joseph (Genesis 41:38-40), Bezaleel (Exodus 35:30, 31), Moses (Numbers 11:16, 17), Joshua (Numbers 27:8-21), Othniel (Judges 3:9, 10), Gideon (Judges 6:34), Jephthah (Judges 11:29), Samson (Judges 13:24, 25), Saul (1 Samuel 10:6).

It was very likely in the light of these examples that the leaders of the Early Church insisted that even those charged with waiting on tables should be filled with the Holy Ghost (Acts 6:3).

(2) *Speakers for God.* The prophet of Israel may be described as a speaker for God—one who received messages from God and passed them on to the people. He was conscious of a heavenly power coming upon him from time to time, enabling him to utter messages not conceived in his own mind, a feature which distinguished him from false prophets (Ezekiel 13:2). The word "prophet" is indicative of inspiration, coming from a word meaning "to bubble up"—a testimony to the torrential outbursts of eloquence which often flowed from the prophet's lips. Compare John 7:38.

(a) The expressions employed to describe the manner in which the inspiration came to them convey the

thought of suddenness and supernaturalness. In referring to the origin of their power, the prophets said
that God poured out the Spirit, gave the Spirit, put
His Spirit upon them, filled them with His Spirit, and
put His Spirit within. Describing the variety of influence, they declared that the Spirit was on them,
rested upon them, laid hold of them. To indicate the
influence exerted on them, they said they were filled
with the Spirit, moved by the Spirit, taken up by the
Spirit, and that the Spirit spoke through them.

(b) When the prophet prophesied he was sometimes in an exalted condition known as "ecstasy"—a
dignified form of the expression "under the power,"
that state of being in which one is lifted above ordinary consciousness and into the spiritual realm, the
realm of prophecy. Ezekiel said, "The hand of the
Lord God (the power of the Lord God) fell there
upon me, . . . and the spirit lifted me up between the
earth and the heaven, and brought me in the visions
of God to Jerusalem" (Ezekiel 8:1-3). It is very likely
that Isaiah was in this condition when he beheld the
glory of Jehovah (Isaiah 6). John the apostle states
that he was "in the Spirit on the Lord's day" (Revelation 1:10; compare Acts 22:17).

The expressions used to describe the inspiration and
ecstasy of the prophets are similar to those describing
the New Testament experience of being filled or baptized with the Spirit (see the Acts). It seems that in
this latter experience the Spirit made so direct an impact on the human spirit that the person was lifted
into a condition of ecstasy, in which condition he gave
utterance to ecstatic speech.

(c) The prophets did not always prophesy in an ecstatic condition; the expression, "the word of the Lord came," implies that the revelation came by a supernatural illumination of the mind. The divine message may be received and delivered in either way.

(d) The prophet did not exercise the gift at his discretion; the prophecy came not "by the will of man" (2 Peter 1:21). Jeremiah said he knew not that people had been plotting against him (Jeremiah 11: 19). The prophets never supposed, nor did Israelites believe, that the power of prophecy was possessed by any man as a constant or uninterrupted gift to be used at will. They understood that the Spirit was a personal agent and that therefore inspiration was by the sovereign will of God. The prophets could, however, bring themselves into a condition of receptivity to the Spirit (2 Kings 3:15), and in times of crisis they could ask God for guidance.

Lesson 5

THE HOLY SPIRIT IN THE OLD TESTAMENT
(Continued)

c. The Regenerative Spirit

We shall considei the following truths relative to the regenerative Spirit. His presence is recorded in the Old Testament, but not emphasized; His bestowal is described mainly as a future blessing; this outpouring is connected with Messiah's coming, and exhibits distinctive features.

(1) *Operative but Not Emphasized.* The Holy Spirit in the Old Testament is also described as being associated with the transformation of human nature. In Isaiah 63:10, 11 reference is made to the Exodus and the wilderness life. When the prophet says that Israel grieved God's Holy Spirit, when it is said that He gave His "good Spirit" to instruct them (Nehemiah 9:20), the reference is to the Spirit as inspiring moral goodness. Compare also Psalm 143:10. David recognized the Spirit as being everywhere, searching out men's ways and throwing the light of God on the darkest recesses of their lives. After his great sin he prayed that God's Holy Spirit, God's sanctifying Presence, the Spirit that influences character, might not be taken from him (Psalm 51:11).

However, this aspect of the Spirit's work is not emphasized in the Old Testament. The name, *Holy* Spirit, occurs only three times in the Old Testament, but 86 times in the New, suggesting that in the Old Testament the emphasis is on the dynamic operations of the Spirit, while in the New the emphasis is upon His sanctifying power.

(2) *Promised as a General Bestowal in the Future.* The general bestowal of the Spirit as the source of holiness is spoken of as an event of the future, one of the blessings of the promised kingdom of God. In Israel the Spirit of God was given to certain chosen leaders, and doubtless wherever there was real godliness it was due to the working of His Spirit. But the mass of the people were generally lapsing into paganism and iniquity, and though revived from time to time through the ministry of prophets and godly kings it became evident that the nation was bad at heart. A general outpouring of the Spirit was needed to turn them back to God.

Such an outpouring was predicted by the prophets, who told of the Spirit being outpoured upon the people in unprecedented measure. Jehovah would cleanse the hearts of the people, put His Spirit within them, and write His law on their inward parts (Ezekiel 36: 25-29; Jeremiah 31:34). In those days the Spirit should be outpoured in power upon all flesh (Joel 2:28), that is, upon all sorts and conditions of men without distinction as to age, sex or rank. Moses' prayer that all of God's people should become prophets would then be fulfilled (Numbers 11:29). As a result many would be converted, for, "whosoever shall call on the name of the Lord shall be delivered" (Joel 2:32).

The distinguishing feature of God's people under the old dispensation was the possession and revelation of the law of God; the distinguishing feature of His people under the new dispensation should be the writing of the law and the abiding of the Spirit in their hearts.

(3) *To Be Connected with Messiah's Coming.* The great outpouring would find its culminating point and climax in the King-Messiah, on whom the Spirit of Jehovah should rest permanently as the Spirit of wisdom and understanding, counsel and might, knowledge and holy fear. He would be the perfect Prophet who should proclaim Good News of liberation, healing, comfort and joy (Isaiah 61:1-3).

What is the connection between these two great events of prophecy—the coming of the Anointed One and the universal effusion of the Holy Spirit? John the Baptist answers: "I indeed baptize you with water unto repentance: but he that cometh after me is mightier than I, whose shoes I am not worthy to bear: he shall baptize you with the Holy Ghost and with fire." In other words, the Messiah is the giver of the Holy Spirit. This is what marked Him as the Messiah or the founder of the kingdom of God; the great blessing of the new age was to be the outpouring of the Spirit and it was Messiah's highest privilege to impart the Spirit. During His earthly ministry Christ spoke of the Spirit as the Father's best gift (Luke 11:13). He invited the spiritually thirsty to come and drink, and offered them an abundant supply of the water of life. In His farewell discourses He promised to send the Comforter to His disciples.

Note especially the connection of the gift with the work of Christ as Redeemer. The giving of the Spirit is connected with Christ's departure (John 16:7) and glorification (John 7:39), which imply His death (John 12:23, 24; 13:31, 33; Luke 24:49). Paul states the connection clearly in Galatians 3:13, 14; Galatians 4:4-6, and Ephesians 1:3, 7, 13, 14.

(4) *Special Features to Be Exhibited.* Perhaps this is the place to enquire concerning the meaning of the statement: "For the Holy Ghost was not yet given; because that Jesus was not yet glorified" (John 7:39). (The word "given" is in italics, indicating that it has been supplied by the translators.) John certainly did not mean that no one in Old Testament times experienced manifestations of the Spirit; every Jew knew that the mighty deeds of Israel's leaders and the messages of the prophets were due to the operations of God's Spirit. He evidently refers to a certain aspect of the Spirit's work which was not known in previous dispensations. What, then, are the distinct features of the Spirit's work in this dispensation?

(a) The Spirit was not yet given as the Spirit of the crucified and glorified Christ. This mission of the Spirit could not begin until the mission of the Son was ended; Jesus could not be manifest in the Spirit until He ceased to live in the flesh. The gift of the Spirit could be claimed by Him for men only when He had taken His place as their Advocate in the presence of God. When Jesus spoke there was as yet no spiritual force in the world such as was brought into it at Pentecost and afterward swept the whole earth like a great tidal wave. For Jesus had not yet returned to where He was before the incarnation (John 6:62), He was not yet with His Father (John 16:7; 20:17); and there

could not be a universal spiritual presence until the
presence in the flesh had been withdrawn, and until
the Son of man had been crowned by His exaltation
to the right hand of God. The Spirit necessarily held
back from this general outpouring of His presence and
power until He could be claimed universally for humanity by a victorious Christ.

(b) In Old Testament times the Spirit was not given
universally but limited generally to Israel and imparted
according to God's sovereign will to certain individuals, such as prophets, priests, kings and other workers in His kingdom. But in this age the Spirit is
available for all regardless of age, sex or race.

In this connection note that in the Old Testament
God's Spirit is rarely referred to by the brief designation, "the Spirit." One reads of "the Spirit of Jehovah"
or "the Spirit of God." But in the New Testament
the brief title, "the Spirit," is of frequent occurrence,
suggesting that His operations are no longer isolated
manifestations but familiar occurrences.

(c) It is believed by some scholars that the impartation of the Spirit in Old Testament times did not
involve the permanent indwelling and abiding which
is characteristic of the New Testament gift. They point
out that the word "gift" implies possession and perma-
nence, and that in this sense there was no *gift* of the
Spirit in the Old Testament.

Yet, the thought that godly individuals were filled
with the Spirit of God in Old Testament times is set
forth clearly in the Scriptures. John the Baptist was
filled with the Holy Ghost from his mother's womb,
and this implies a permanent anointing (Luke 1:15) .

And further, John belonged to the old dispensation; in fact, he never came into the place of greater privilege in the "kingdom of heaven" (the spiritual kingdom) made possible by the sacrificial death of his cousin by blood relationship and his Lord by rank. Yet *he* was permanently "filled with the Spirit."

Shall we say that the Old Testament prophets Elijah, Elisha, Isaiah, Jeremiah, Ezekiel, Daniel, and other godly men and women did not have the *abiding* presence of the Spirit? Take the experience of the prophet Ezekiel for an example. The Spirit of God was most active in the induction of this wonderfully and uniquely consecrated man into the prophetic office and was in complete control of his life afterwards in his extraordinary pantomimic ministry. Compare Ezekiel 3:12; 3:24 ("the Spirit entered into me") and 3:25-27. Note the control of the Spirit over this man in this latter passage.

The distinction between Old and New Testament experiences seems to be, not that the Spirit came only for special occasions upon godly men and then left them, but that the Old Testament operation of the Spirit was *individualistic* as compared with the *universality* of his availability in the new dispensation ushered in by the completion of Christ's redemptive work and His subsequent glorification. Compare "all flesh"—Joel 2:28, 29.

Further distinction may be seen from the New Testament order in the additional sign of speaking with tongues accompanying the filling of the Spirit. Compare Isaiah 28:11, 12; 1 Corinthians 14:21; Mark 16:17.

Lesson 6

THE HOLY SPIRIT IN CHRIST

The New Testament ushered in the Dispensation of the Spirit, fulfilling the promise that God would pour out of His Spirit on all flesh, put His Spirit within His people's hearts, and so write His laws there. This was to be done in the days of the Messiah, who was to be anointed with the Holy Spirit. Accordingly we find in the New Testament that the Holy Spirit is represented as working upon, in and through Jesus Christ.

The designations, "Spirit of Christ," "Spirit of Jesus Christ," indicate a relation between Christ and the Holy Spirit which is not shared by His disciples. For example, we would not think of speaking of the "Spirit of Paul."

From the beginning to the end of His earthly life the Lord Jesus was intimately connected with the Holy Spirit. So close is the connection that Paul describes Christ as a "quickening Spirit." The meaning is not that Jesus is the Spirit, but that He gives the Spirit and through the same Spirit exercises omnipresence.

The Spirit is mentioned in connection with the following crises and aspects of Christ's ministry:

a. At His Birth

The Holy Spirit is described as the agent in the miraculous conception of Jesus (Matthew 1:20; Luke 1:35). Jesus was in relation with the Spirit of God

from the first moment of His human existence. The
Holy Spirit came upon Mary, the Power of the Most
High overshadowed her, and that which was born of
her was entitled to be called holy, Son of God. For
John the forerunner it sufficed that he be filled with
the Holy Ghost from his mother's womb, whereas Jesus
was to be conceived by the power of the Spirit in the
womb and for that reason to bear names and titles
such as could not be given to John. God, working by
His Spirit, is the Father of the humanity of Jesus in
the sense that its origination from the substance of
the virgin mother was a divine act.

The effect of this divine intervention is seen in
Christ's sinlessness, His entire consecration, His uninterrupted sense of the Fatherhood of God. The power
of sin was broken at last, and One born of a woman
was, even as a man, holy and a Son of God. The second Man is from heaven (1 Corinthians 15:47). His
life was from above (John 8:23); its course was a
victory over sin and its issues in the quickening of the
race (1 Corinthians 15:45). He who has no sin and
saves His people from their sin must needs have been
begotten of the Holy Ghost.

b. In the Anointing at His Baptism

As years went by a fresh relation with the Spirit
began. He who had been conceived of the Spirit and
conscious of the divine indwelling, was anointed with
the Spirit. As in the conception the Spirit descended upon Mary, so at the baptism the Spirit descended upon
her Son anointing Him to be Prophet, Priest and King.
The first operation sanctified His humanity; the sec-

ond consecrated His official life. As His conception was the beginning of His human existence, so His baptism was the beginning of His active ministry.

c. Throughout His Ministry

Then He was led by the Spirit into the wilderness (Mark 1:12) to be tempted by Satan. Here He overcame those suggestions of the prince of this world that would have led Him to attempt His work in a selfish, vainglorious and worldly spirit, and to use His power along natural lines.

He carried on His ministry in the consciousness of the indwelling of the divine power. He knew that the Spirit of the Lord God was upon Him to fulfill the ministry predicted of the Messiah (Luke 4:18); by the finger of God He cast out demons (Luke 11:20; compare Acts 10:38). He testified to the fact that the Father within Him performed the miraculous works.

d. In the Crucifixion

The same Spirit who led Him into the wilderness and sustained Him there, also gave Him strength to consummate His ministry upon the cross, where "through the eternal Spirit he offered himself without spot unto God" (Hebrews 9:14). He went to the cross with the anointing still upon Him. The Spirit kept before Him the inflexible claims of God and enflamed Him with love for man and zeal for God, to go forward in spite of hindrance, pain and difficulty to effect the world's redemption. The Holy Spirit filled His mind with unflagging ardor, zeal and love which led Him to complete His sacrifice. His human spirit was so penetrated and elevated by the Spirit of God that it lived in the eternal and invisible, and was able to "endure the cross, despising the shame."

e. In His Resurrection

The Holy Spirit was the quickening agent in Christ's resurrection (Romans 1:4; 8:11). Some days after this event Christ appeared unto His disciples, breathed on them and said, "Receive ye the Holy Ghost" (John 20: 22; compare Acts 1:2). These words cannot mean the enduement of power for which the Lord, before His ascension, had commanded them to tarry. Some students believe that the breathing was merely symbolic of what was to occur 50 days hence; that is, a reminder of the coming Pentecost. Others believe that something definite was imparted to the disciples.

A comparison with Genesis 2:7 indicates that the divine inbreathing symbolized a creative act. Christ is later described as a quickening or life-giving Spirit (1 Corinthians 15:45). May it not be that on this occasion the Lord of life made these disciples to know by experience "the power of his resurrection"? The eleven were to be sent into the world to fulfill a new commission; they were to continue the work of Christ. Of such a mission they were in themselves incapable, just as an inanimate body is incapable of performing the functions of a living man. Hence the act symbolizing the giving of life. As the old humanity was inbreathed by the Lord God, so the new humanity is inbreathed by the Lord Christ.

If we grant a real impartation on this occasion it must be remembered, however, that it is not the Person of the Comforter but the inspiration of His life which was communicated. Bishop Wescott thus states the distinction between the "Gift of Easter" and the "Gift of Pentecost"—"The one answers to the power of the Resurrection, and the other to the power of the Ascension." That is, the one is the grace of quickening, and the other is the grace of endowment.

f. Related to the Ascension

Note the following three degrees in the impartation of the Spirit to Christ: (1) At His conception the Spirit of God was from that moment the Spirit of Jesus, the vivifying, sanctifying power by which He entered on His life as the Son of man and lived it to the end. (2) As years went by a fresh relation with the Spirit began. The Spirit of God became the Spirit of Christ in the sense of resting upon Him for His Christ-ministry. (3) After the ascension the Spirit became the Spirit of Christ in the sense of being imparted by Him to others.

The Spirit came to abide upon Christ not only for His own needs, but also that He might bestow Him upon all believers. (See John 1:33 and note especially the word "remaining.") After the ascension the Lord Jesus exercised the great prerogative given Him as Messiah—the sending of the Spirit upon others (Acts 2:33; compare Revelation 5:6). Hence He gives the blessing that He Himself has received and enjoys, and makes us joint-partakers with Himself. Thus we read not only of the gift but the "communion" of the Holy Spirit, that is, partaking in common of the privilege and blessing of having the Spirit of God given to us. It is not only fellowship of believers with one another

but also with Christ; they receive the same anointing
as He did; it is like the precious anointing on the
head of Aaron, that flowed down his beard and descended even to the skirts of his garments. All the
members of Christ's body, as a kingdom of priests,
partake of the anointing of the Spirit flowing from its
Head, our great High Priest, who has passed into the
heavens.

Lesson 7

THE HOLY SPIRIT IN HUMAN EXPERIENCE

This section concerns itself with the varied operations of the Spirit in relation to the individual.

a. Conviction

In John 16:7-11 Jesus describes the work of the Comforter in relation to the world. The Spirit will act as Christ's prosecuting attorney, so to speak, working to secure a divine conviction against the rejectors of Christ. To convict means to bring home truths otherwise doubted or discarded; or to bring home charges made against conduct and life. Men do not know what sin, righteousness and judgment really are, and therefore need to be convinced of spiritual truth. For example, it would be useless to argue with a person who declared he could see no beauty in a rose, for his inability would argue lack of appreciation of beauty. A sense of beauty must be awakened within him; he must be convinced of the beauty of the flower. In like manner, the darkened mind and soul sees nothing in spiritual truths until convinced and awakened by the Holy Spirit. He will convince men of the following truths:

(1) *The Sin of Unbelief.* When Peter preached on the Day of Pentecost he had nothing to say of the people's looseness of life, their worldliness, their covetousness. He did not go into details of their depravity

in order to bring a blush of shame to their cheeks. *The* sin he charged them with, and commanded them to repent of, was the crucifixion of the Lord of glory. The peril he warned them against was the refusal to believe on Him in the face of evidence.

The sin of unbelief is here described as the only sin because, in the words of one scholar, "where it continues all other sins are retained, and when it departs all other sins are removed." It is the mother sin because it produces new sins and because it is the sin against the remedy for sin. Writes Dr. Smeaton, "But however great and perilous this sin may be, such is the ignorance in which man is naturally involved, that its criminality is utterly unknown till it is brought home by the influence of the Holy Ghost, the Comforter. Conscience may convince a man of ordinary sins, but never of the sin of unbelief. Of the enormity of this sin no man was ever convinced but by the Holy Ghost Himself."

(2) *The Righteousness of Christ.* "Of righteousness, because I go to my Father, and ye see me no more." Jesus Christ was crucified as a malefactor and a deceiver of the people. But after the Day of Pentecost, the outpouring of the Spirit and the performing of miracles in His name convinced thousands of Jews that He was not only righteous but also the only heavenly source and way of righteousness. Through Peter the Spirit convinced them that they had crucified the Lord of righteousness (Acts 2:36, 37), but He also assured them that there was pardon and salvation in His name (Acts 2:38).

(3) *The Judgment of Satan.* "Of judgment, because

the prince of this world is judged." How are people today convinced that crime will be judged and punished? By the exposure of the criminal and his subsequent punishment; in other words, by a demonstration of justice. The Cross was a demonstration of the truth that the power of Satan over the lives of men was broken, and that his complete destruction was decreed (Hebrews 2:14, 15; 1 John 3:8; Colossians 2:15; Romans 16:20). Satan has been judged in the sense that the great cause has gone against him so that he has no more right to hold men in bondage as his subjects. By His death Christ has delivered all men from Satan's dominion, and it remains for them to accept their deliverance. Men are convinced by the Holy Spirit that they are free indeed (John 8:36), no more subjects of the tempter, no more bound to obey him, but loyal subjects of Christ and made willing in the day of His power (Psalm 110:3).

Satan contended that he had a right to possess men who had sinned and that the righteous Judge must leave them in his hands. The Mediator, on the other hand, appealed to the fact that He bore man's penalty and took his place, therefore justice as well as mercy required that Satan's right of conquest should be reversed and that the world should be given to Him who was its second Adam and Lord of all. The verdict was given against the prince of this world—and he was judged. He can no longer keep his goods in peace when the stronger than he comes upon the scene (Luke 11:21, 22).

b. Regeneration

The creative work of the Spirit upon the soul may

be illustrated by the creative work of God's Spirit upon man's body in the beginning. Picture the scene suggested by Genesis 2:7. God takes the dust of the earth and forms a body. There it lies, inanimate and still. Though in the world and surrounded by its beauties it does not react, because it has no life. It neither sees nor hears nor understands. Then "God breathed into his nostrils the breath of life; and man became a living soul." At once he reacted to the world, saw its beauties and heard its sounds.

As with the body, so with the soul. Man is surrounded by the spirit world and by God who is not far from any of us (Acts 17:27). Yet he lives and acts as if that world did not exist, because he is spiritually dead and therefore cannot react to it. But when the same Lord who quickened the body quickens the soul, the person awakens to the spiritual world and begins to live the spiritual life. Anyone who has witnessed the reactions of a genuine convert following the thoroughgoing experience called the new birth knows that regeneration is not merely a doctrine but a practical reality.

c. Indwelling

See John 14:17; Romans 8:9; 1 Corinthians 6:19; 2 Timothy 1:14; 1 John 2:27; Colossians 1:27; 1 John 3:24; Revelation 3:20.

God is always and necessarily present everywhere; in Him all men live, move and have their being. But indwelling means that He is present in a new way, sustaining a *personal* relation to the individual. This union with God, which is called indwelling, is produced in reality by the presence of the whole Trinity,

as will be seen by an examination of the above texts.
But since it is the special ministry of the Holy Spirit
to indwell the hearts of men, the experience is commonly known as the indwelling of the Holy Spirit. It
is believed by many orthodox scholars that God imparted to Adam not only physical and mental life, but
also the indwelling Spirit, which he lost because of
sin, not only for himself but also for his descendants.
This absence of the Spirit has left man in spiritual
darkness and weakness. In relation to understanding,
the unconverted cannot know the things of the Spirit
of God (1 Corinthians 2:14). In relation to the will,
he cannot be subject to the law of God (Romans 8:
7). In relation to worship, he cannot call Jesus "Lord"
(1 Corinthians 12:3). As regards practice, he cannot
please God (Romans 8:8). In regard to character, he
cannot bear spiritual fruit (John 15:4). In regard to
faith, he cannot receive the spirit of truth (John 14:
17). All this is due to the absence of the Spirit, an
absence which leaves man in spiritual death.

By faith and repentance man turns to God and becomes regenerated. Regeneration by the Spirit involves
a union with God and Christ (1 Corinthians 6:17)
which is known as indwelling (1 Corinthians 6:19).
This indwelling of the Spirit or man's possession of
the Spirit is the mark of a New Testament Christian.
"But ye are not in the flesh, but in the Spirit, if so
be that the Spirit of God dwell in you. Now if any
man have not the Spirit of Christ, he is none of his"
(Romans 8:9; compare Jude 19).

Writes Dr. Smeaton:

"We must hold on the sure ground of Scripture that

not only are the gifts of the Spirit poured into the hearts of believers, but the personal Holy Ghost, who had left man's heart in ruins, and no longer His temple, returns to take up His abode in the redeemed, and occupies them with a personal, hidden, indwelling presence which our limited faculties in this transitory state do not permit us to measure or to comprehend. Enough that the fact is plainly taught us in the Holy Scriptures, however incapable we may be to grasp or explain it to ourselves or to other minds."

One of the most comprehensive definitions of a Christian is that he is a man in whom the Holy Spirit dwells. His body is a temple of the Holy Ghost, in virtue of which experience he is sanctified as the Tabernacle was consecrated by Jehovah's indwelling. He is then called a "saint," and it becomes his duty to guard the sanctity of the temple of his body. Compare 1 Corinthians 6:19 and Romans 12:1.

d. Sanctification

In regeneration the Holy Spirit effects a radical change in the soul by imparting a new principle of life. But this does not imply that the child of God is at once perfect. There remain inherited and acquired weaknesses. There are still the world, the flesh and the devil to overcome.

Since the Spirit does not work magically, but in a vital and progressive manner, it is by degrees that the soul is renewed. Faith must be strengthened through many tests; love must be fortified to survive hardship and temptation. Allurements to sin must be overcome; tendencies and habits must be corrected.

If the Spirit of God did one work and then departed, the convert would indeed fall back into his old ways. But the Spirit continues the good work He has begun. The gospel, which was the means of our new birth, continues to be the means of growth in our Christian life. Those who have been born by the incorruptible seed of the Word of God (1 Peter 1:23) must, "as newborn babes, desire the sincere milk of the word, that ye may grow thereby" (1 Peter 2:2). Also, the Holy Spirit acts directly upon the soul producing those special virtues of Christian character known as the fruit of the Spirit (Galatians 5:22, 23). The operation of the Spirit is progressive, going "from the heart to the surface, from the interior to the exterior, from the seat of life to the manifestations of life, to the actions and to the words; at first allowing many things which are incompatible with His holy nature, then, little by little, attacking them one after another, one year these, another year those, going into all the details so thoroughly that, nothing being able to escape His influence, one day the entire man, glorified by the Spirit, will be resplendent with the life of God."

Lesson 8

THE HOLY SPIRIT IN HUMAN EXPERIENCE
(Continued)

e. Enduement with Power

In this section we shall consider the following facts concerning the enduement of power: its general character, its special character, its initial evidence, its continuous aspect, and the manner of its reception.

(1) *Its General Nature.* The foregoing sections have dealt with the regenerative and sanctifying work of the Holy Spirit. In this section we shall deal with another mode of operation, His energizing work. This last phase of the Spirit's work is set forth in Christ's promise: "But ye shall receive power, after that the Holy Ghost is come upon you: and ye shall be witnesses unto me" (Acts 1:8).

(a) The main feature of this promise is power for service and not regeneration for eternal life. Whenever we read of the Spirit coming upon, resting upon, falling upon, or filling people, the reference is never to the saving work of the Spirit but always to power for service.

(b) The words were addressed to men already in intimate relationship with Christ. They had been sent out to preach, armed with spiritual power for that purpose (Matthew 10:1). To them it was said, "Your names are written in heaven" (Luke 10:20). Their moral condition was described in the words, "Now ye are clean through the word which I have spoken unto you" (John 15:3). Their relationship to Christ was illustrated by the figure, "I am the vine, ye are the branches" (John 15:5). They knew the presence of the Spirit with them (John 14:17); they had felt the breath of the risen Christ and heard Him say, "Receive ye the Holy Ghost" (John 20:22).

The above facts show that one may be in touch with Christ and be a disciple of Christ and yet lack the special enduement of power mentioned in Acts 1:8. It may be objected that all this relates to the disciples before Pentecost; but in Acts 8:12-16 we have an instance of people baptized into Christ, who received the gift of the Spirit some days later.

(c) Accompanying the fulfillment of this promise (Acts 1:8) were supernatural manifestations (Acts 2: 1-4), the most important and common of which was the miraculous utterance in other languages. That this supernatural utterance was an accompaniment of the receiving of spiritual power as stated in two other instances (Acts 10:44-46; 19:1-6) and implied in another (Acts 8:14-19).

(d) This impartation is described as a baptism (Acts 1:5). When the word "baptism" is applied to spiritual experience, it is used figuratively to describe immersion in the energizing power of the divine Spirit. The word was used figuratively by Christ to describe His immersion in the floods of suffering (Matthew 20:22).

(e) This impartation of power is also described as

a filling with the Spirit. Those who were baptized with the Holy Spirit on the Day of Pentecost were also filled with the Spirit.

(2) *Its Special Characteristic.* The above facts lead us to conclude that in addition and subsequent to conversion, a believer (may) experience an enduement of power whose initial oncoming is signalized by a miraculous utterance in a language never learned by the speaker.

The above conclusion has been challenged. It is claimed that there are many Christians who know the Holy Spirit in regenerating and sanctifying power, and yet have not spoken in other tongues. Indeed, the New Testament teaches that one cannot be a Christian without having the Spirit, which is the same as being indwelt by the Spirit. "If any man have not the Spirit of Christ, he is none of his" (Romans 8:9). That the Spirit of Christ means the Holy Spirit is indicated by the context and proved by 1 Peter 1:11 where "Spirit of Christ" can refer only to the Holy Spirit. Other references are cited as supporting the same truth (Romans 5:5; 8:14, 16; 1 Corinthians 6:19; Galatians 4:6; 1 John 3:24; 4:13). It is also affirmed that many Christian workers have experienced anointings of the Spirit by which they have been enabled to win people to Christ and to do other Christian work, and yet these same workers have not spoken in other tongues.

It cannot be successfully denied that there is a real sense in which all truly regenerated persons have the Spirit, but the question naturally follows: What is there different and additional in the experience described as the baptism with the Holy Spirit? We answer as follows:

There is one Holy Spirit, but many operations of that Spirit, just as there is one electricity but many operations of that electricity. The same electricity propels street cars, lights our houses, operates refrigerators, and performs many other tasks. In like manner, the one Spirit regenerates, sanctifies, energizes, illumines, and imparts special gifts.

The Spirit regenerates human nature in the crisis of conversion and then, as the Spirit of holiness within, produces the "fruit of the Spirit," the distinctive features of Christian character. At times, believers make a special consecration, and receive victory over sin, and consequent accession of joy and peace.

But in addition to these operations of the Holy Spirit there is another, having for its special purpose the energizing of human nature for special service for God, and issuing in an outward expression of a supernatural character. In a general way, Paul refers to this outward expression as "the manifestation of the Spirit" (1 Corinthians 12:7), perhaps in contrast to the quiet and secret operations of the Spirit. In the New Testament this experience is designated by such expressions as falling upon, coming upon, being poured out, being filled with, which expressions convey the thought of suddenness and supernaturalness. All these terms are connected with the experience known as the baptism with the Holy Spirit (Acts 1:5).

The operation of the Spirit described by these terms

is so distinct from His quiet and ordinary manifestations that scholars have coined a word to describe it. That word is "charismatic," from a Greek word frequently used to designate a special impartation of spiritual power. Wrote A. B. Bruce, a Presbyterian scholar:

"The Spirit's work was conceived of as transcendent, miraculous, and charismatic. The power of the Holy Ghost was a power coming from without, producing extraordinary effects that could arrest the attention of even a profane eye like that of Simon the sorcerer."

While acknowledging that the early Christians believed also in the sanctifying operations of the Spirit (he cites Acts 16:14), and His inspiring of faith, hope, and love within people, he concludes that "the gift of the Holy Spirit came to mean ... the power to speak ecstatically, and to prophesy enthusiastically, and to heal the sick by a word of prayer."

The point we desire to emphasize is that the baptism with the Holy Spirit, which is a baptism of power, is charismatic in character, judging from the descriptions of the results of the impartation.

Now while freely admitting that Christians have been born of the Spirit, and workers anointed with the Spirit, we maintain that not all Christians have experienced the charismatic operation of the Spirit followed by a sudden, supernatural utterance.

(3) *Its Initial Evidence.* How do we know when a person receives the charismatic impartation of the Holy Spirit? In other words, what is the evidence that one has experienced the baptism with the Holy Spirit? The question cannot be decided from the four Gospels,

because they contain prophecies of the coming of the
Spirit, and a prophecy is made perfectly clear only by
fulfillment. Neither can it be settled by the Epistles,
for they are largely pastoral instructions addressed to
established churches where the power of the Spirit
with outward manifestations was considered the normal
experience of every Christian. It is therefore evident
that the matter must be settled by the Book of Acts
which records many instances of people's receiving the
baptism with the Spirit, and describes the results that
followed.

We grant that the results of the impartation are not
recorded in every case mentioned in the Book of Acts,
but where the results are described there is always an
immediate, supernatural, outward expression, convinc-
ing not only the receiver but also the people listening
to him that a divine power is controlling the person.
In every case there is an ecstatic speaking in a language
that the person has never learned.

Is the above statement merely the private interpretation of one religious group or is it recognized by
others? Dr. Rees, an English theologian of liberal views,
writes:

"Glossolalia (speaking in tongues) was the most con-
spicuous and popular gift of the early years of the
church. It seems to have been the regular accompaniment and evidence of the descent of the Spirit upon
believers."

Writes Dr. G. B. Stevens of Yale, in his *Theology
of the New Testament*:

"The Spirit was regarded as a special gift which did not always accompany baptism and faith. The Samaritans were not regarded as having the Holy Ghost when they believed the Word of God. They had believed and had been baptized, but it was only when Peter and John laid their hands upon them that the gift of the Spirit was bestowed. Evidently some special endowment or experience is here in view."

Commenting on Acts 19:1-7 he writes:

"Not only did they not receive the Holy Ghost when they believed, but after they had been baptized in the name of Christ it was only when Paul had laid his hands upon them that the Holy Ghost came upon them and they spoke with tongues and prophesied. Here it is obvious that the gift of the Spirit is regarded as synonymous with the ecstatic charismata (spiritual impartation) of speaking with tongues and prophesying."

Writes Dr. A. B. Macdonald, a Scotch Presbyterian minister:

"The church's belief in the Spirit sprang from her experience of a fact. Very early in her career the disciples became aware of a new power working within them. Its most striking manifestation at first was 'speaking in tongues,' the power of ecstatic utterance in an unintelligible speech; and both those seized by this power and those who saw and heard its manifestations were convinced that some Power from a higher world had broken into their lives, endowing them with capacities of utterance and with other gifts, which appeared to be something different from a mere heightening of endowments already theirs. People who hitherto had seemed to be nothing out of common suddenly became capable of impassioned prayer and speech, or of lofty moods in which they were manifestly holding converse with the Unseen."

He states that the speaking in tongues "appears to have been the most arresting and at first the most characteristic of the manifestations of the Spirit."

Scripture Proof of "Initial Evidence"

It is well to establish a definite scriptural foundation for believing that the initial evidence of the reception of the baptism in the Spirit is the speaking with tongues.

Where would be the logical place in Scripture to look to establish this teaching? The Gospels? It is true that the Spirit was promised in these records. Cf. Matthew 3:11; John 14:16, 26; 16:13, 14. Yet, not here. The Epistles? In the Epistles there is a wide scope of teaching regarding the Holy Spirit in His various operations in the Church, but this is largely of a doctrinal and explanatory nature. No, not here.

The answer to the question is, "In the Book of Acts," for there are recorded the different instances of the dynamic manifestations of the Spirit, His objective movings, dispensationally as on Pentecost and later in the cases of different groups. In the Gospels we read of the Spirit in promise; in the Epistles we discover His subjective work in sanctification and His operations in the Church; but in the Acts His *dynamic objective* work in the early history of the Church. Here we shall find the evidence we seek.

While there were accompaniments of the presence and power of the Spirit on the Day of Pentecost other than tongues—"the rushing mighty wind," "the cloven tongues like as of fire"—the particular sign of tongues was manifest not only then, but on later occasions also.

The pattern of the receiving of the Spirit at Pentecost was clearly the glossolalia (Acts 2:4).

STUDY QUESTIONS—UNIT ONE

LESSON ONE

1. What is the true significance of the "Pentecostal Movement" from the negative standpoint?
2. From the positive standpoint?
3. What prominence does the doctrine of the Holy Spirit take in the Scripture? Be explicit.
4. How does neglect of this doctrine of the Holy Spirit affect the church?
5. Prove the deity of the Holy Spirit from scriptural facts.
6. Why is the Holy Spirit sometimes wrongly thought to be only impersonal influence?
7. Prove the personality of the Holy Spirit in four ways.
8. What is the relationship of the Holy Spirit to the Father?

LESSON TWO

1. Give reasons for the designation of the Holy Spirit as "the Spirit of Christ."
2. What is the significance of the name "Comforter"?
3. Give the significance of the word "another" in Christ's promise of the Comforter.
4. Tell something of the special relationship between Christ and the Holy Spirit.
5. Show the advantages of Christ's return to the Father and the coming of the Holy Spirit.
6. Give the significance of the name "Holy Spirit."

7. "The Holy Spirit of Promise."
8. "The Spirit of Truth."
9. "The Spirit of Grace."
10. "The Spirit of Life."
11. "The Spirit of Adoption."

LESSON THREE

1. Give proof texts of the unity of God.
2. Show that this unity is a compound one.
3. What manifestation of the divine Being in the Old Testament revealed Him in bodily form? Give instances of its occurrence.
4. Show from Matthew 3:16, 17 and Matthew 28:19 evidence of the doctrine of the Trinity.
5. Give Boardman's statement of the doctrine.
6. Show how the equilateral triangle illustrates the doctrine of tri-unity.
7. Do the same with light.
8. Quote several scriptures other than in Matthew where the three Persons are mentioned.
9. Show the reasonableness of the relationship of Father and Son on a plane of equality.

LESSON FOUR

1. Look up the meaning of the word "symbol."
2. Explain the import of the symbol of fire as applied to the Holy Spirit.
3. Wind.
4. Water.

5. A seal.
6. Oil.
7. The Dove.
8. In what three ways is the Holy Spirit revealed in the Old Testament?
9. Tell something of His work as the Creative Spirit.
10. As the Dynamc Spirit.
11. How is the operation of the Holy Spirit seen in empowering workers for God?
12. Tell all you can of His activities in relation to the prophets.

LESSON FIVE

1. Give some indications from Scripture of the operations of the Holy Spirit in the Old Testament.
2. How is He revealed in relation to the future?
3. How is He connected with the coming of Messiah?
4. Give some distinctions between the ministry and operation of the Holy Spirit in the Old Testament times and those in the New Testament.

LESSON SIX

1. Explain the relationship of the Holy Spirit to the birth of Christ and to His sinlessness.
2. Explain the event of the descent of the dove at Christ's baptism in Jordan.
3. How was the Holy Spirit related to the ministry of Jesus?
4. To His crucifixion?

5. To His resurrection?
6. To Him as ascended to heaven?

LESSON SEVEN

1. Explain the work of the Holy Spirit as Christ's prosecuting attorney.
2. Of what does He convict?
3. State something concerning each point.
4. Illustrate the work of the Holy Spirit in regeneration.
5. Tell all you can of the Holy Spirit as the Indweller of the believer.
6. Explain the meaning of sanctification and how the Holy Spirit operates to sanctify us.

LESSON EIGHT

1. What is the main feature of the enduement with power by the Holy Spirit?
2. To whom was this promise primarily given?
3. How was this power displayed?
4. What is the meaning of the word baptism as applied to the experience of being filled with the Spirit?
5. Tell some of the special characteristics accompanying the enduement with power.
6. What do we mean by "charismatic" as related to the baptism with the Spirit?
7. What is the initial evidence of the baptism with the Spirit?
8. Where should we logically look for scriptural proof that this is the initial evidence?
9. Prove the initial evidence from the Word.

UNIT TWO

Lessons 9 to 12

Lesson 9

THE HOLY SPIRIT IN HUMAN EXPERIENCE
(Continued)

In the account of the revival in Samaria (Acts 8: 5-25) there is no specific mention of tongues accompanying the baptism which was received through apostolic imposition of hands (verses 14-17), but other evidences of such an outward sign are clearly present. Simon, the sorcerer, seeing the miracles which were performed through Philip, apparently believed and was baptized. Evidently before Philip's coming he had displayed some sort of miraculous power, for they called him "the great power of God."

When the believers received the Holy Ghost by the laying on of the apostles' hands, Simon *saw* something occur, which aroused his covetousness, and he offered Peter and John money that he might have the same power. A man of Simon's type certainly would not offer money to be able to produce an effect not visible.

Who can consistently deny that Simon witnessed the glossolalia? Many eminent commentators and theologians confirm this view.

The bigoted apostle Peter, whose Jewish prejudices the Lord had to resolve drastically before he even started on his mission to Caesarea, had the clearest demonstration anyone could desire that God was making no distinction between the Jews and the Gentiles. For while Peter preached Christ to Cornelius' household (Acts 10:34-48), "the Spirit fell on all them that heard the word" and Peter and the other Jews who had accompanied him were "astonished" because they "heard them speak with tongues and magnify God." This was all the proof they needed, as Peter later testified twice in Jerusalem before his countrymen (Acts 11:15-18; 15:7, 8), that the Spirit had fallen on these Gentile believers "as on us at the beginning."

Is it difficult to believe that the "basically similar experience at Jerusalem and Caesarea revealed God's plan for the experience throughout this whole dispensation in which there is 'neither Jew nor Greek' "?
—Brumback.

Then there is the incident of the appearance of tongues at Ephesus (Acts 19:1-7). Again, God employed tongues as a supernatural sign of the infilling of these men with the Holy Ghost.

It is intensely interesting to note how individuals of various racial and religious classes are all led in the plan of God to the same point in the progress of spiritual experience. By this procedure He established that climax of experience as the pattern of a full normal scriptural Christian experience. Let us examine the record.

There were the twelve, located in the sunset of the dispensation of law and in the sunrise of the new dispensation of grace, who were brought to the experience of Pentecost with the accompanying signs of tongues. They had been taught personally by the Lord, and were declared by Christ, with the exception of Judas, to be "clean through the Word which I have spoken unto you."

There were the Samaritans, of hybrid race, despised by the Jews and in turn despising them, receiving the baptism of the Spirit (obviously with the same sign).

There were also the Gentile "dogs" at Caesarea, "aliens from the commonwealth of Israel and strangers from the covenants of promise," saved and filled with the Spirit with the same sign of tongues.

Then follow the pagan Ephesians, probably proselytes to the Jewish religion, who may have been at Jerusalem at some time for a Jewish feast. They had been baptized unto repentance, but had not heard of the subsequent momentous events; now we see them receiving Christ as Saviour and being sealed with the Spirit, and speaking with tongues.

All these various classes arrived at the same point of normal early-church experience of being "filled with

the Spirit." Who can honestly contradict that this has
been God's purpose for every believer during this
church era?

Spiritual Manifestations Since Pentecost

Various post-apostolic fathers of the Church such
as Irenaeus, Tertullian, Justin Martyr, Origen, all tes-
tify in language similar to Chrysostom, golden-mouthed
preacher of Constantinople (4th century A.D.) : "Whoever was baptized in apostolic days, he straightway
spake with tongues, . . . and one straightway spake in
the Persian language, another in the Roman, another
in the Indian, another in some other tongue, and this
made manifest to them that were without that it was
the Spirit in the very person speaking."

There is not sufficient space in a course of this com-
pass for an extended discussion of the recurrence of
this phenomenon in the history of the church since
the early days, but the following quotation from the
Encyclopaedia Britannica sums it up well: "The glossolalia recurs in Christian revivals of every age; e.g.,
among the mendicant friars of the thirteenth century,
among the Jensenists, and early Quakers, the converts
of Wesley and Whitefield, the persecuted Protestants
of the Cevennes, and the Irvingites" (vol. 27, pages
9, 10, 11th edition) .

Is there any place in the New Testament where a
distinction is made between those who have received
the enduement of power and those who have not?
A. B. Macdonald, the writer quoted earlier, answers

in the affirmative. He points out that the word "unlearned" in 1 Corinthians 14:16, 23 (which he translates, "private Christian") denotes persons who are differentiated from unbelievers by the fact that they take part in the worship to the extent of saying "Amen"; they also are distinguished from believers by the fact that they are unable to take active part in Spirit-manifestations. It seems that a special section in the meetinghouse was reserved for the "unlearned ones" (1 Corinthians 14:16).

Weymouth translates the word "unlearned" by the expression, "some who lack the gift." Thayer's lexicon renders it: "one who is destitute of the gift of tongues; a Christian who is not a prophet." Macdonald describes him as "one who waits, or is kept waiting, for the decisive moment when the Spirit will descend upon him."

Regardless of their denomination or school of theological thought, able scholars agree that the receiving of the Spirit in the Early Church was no formal ceremony or doctrinal theory, but a real experience. Canon Streeter says that Paul asks the Galatians whether it was by the law or by the hearing of faith that they received the gift of the Spirit, "as if the reception of the Spirit was something as definite and observable as, for example, an attack of influenza."

(4) *Its Continuous Aspect.* The experience described as being "filled with the Spirit" is connected with the thought of power for service. Three phases of this experience are to be distinguished:

(a) The initial filling when a person is for the first time baptized with the Holy Spirit.

(b) A habitual condition as referred to in the words, "full of the Holy Ghost" (Acts 6:3; 7:55; 11:24). These words describe the daily life of a spiritual person, or one whose character reveals "the fruit of the Spirit." The habitual condition is referred to in the exhortation, "Be filled with the Spirit" (Ephesians 5:18).

(c) Fillings or anointings for special occasions. Paul was filled with the Holy Spirit after his conversion, but in Acts 13:9 we learn that God gave him a special enduement wherewith to resist the evil power of a sorcerer. Peter was filled with the Spirit on the Day of Pentecost, but God granted a special anointing when he stood before the Jewish council (Acts 4:8). The disciples had received the infilling or Baptism with the Spirit on the Day of Pentecost, but in answer to prayer God gave them a special enduement to fortify them against the opposition of the Jewish leaders (Acts 4:31). As the late F. B. Meyer once said:

You may be a man full of the Holy Ghost in your family, but before entering the pulpit be sure that you are especially equipped by a new reception of the Holy Ghost.

(5) *The Manner of Its Reception.* How may one receive this baptism of power?

(a) A right attitude is essential. The first group to experience the oncoming of the Spirit "continued with one accord in prayer and supplication" (Acts 1:14).

Ideally, one should receive the enduement of power immediately after conversion, but actually there may be circumstances of one kind or another which make tarrying necessary.

(b) The receiving of the gift of the Holy Spirit subsequent to conversion is connected with the prayers of Christian workers. The writer of Acts thus describes the experience of the Samaritan converts who had already believed and had been baptized: "Who, when they [Peter and John] were come down, prayed for them, that they might receive the Holy Ghost.... Then laid they their hands on them, and they received the Holy Ghost" (Acts 8:15, 17) .

Weinel, a German theologian, made a thorough study of the spiritual manifestations during the apostolic age. He says that "what might be called 'inspirational sessions' were held till well on into the second century, strange as they seem to outsiders." The Holy Ghost, he states, was communicated to converts by the laying on of hands and prayer, and wrought signs and wonders. "Inspirational sessions" would seem to describe special services for those who desired to receive the Spirit's power.

(c) The receiving of spiritual power is connected with the united prayers of the church. After the Christians of the church at Jerusalem had prayed for boldness to preach the Word, "the place was shaken where they were assembled together; and they were all filled with the Holy Ghost" (Acts 4:31) . The expression "place was shaken" implies something spectacular and supernatural which convinced the disciples that the power which descended on the Day of Pentecost was still present in the church.

(d) A spontaneous outpouring may, in some cases, make prayer or effort unnecessary as was the case with those in the house of Cornelius, whose hearts had already been "purified by faith" (Acts 10:44; 15: 9).

(e) Since the baptism of power is described as a gift (Acts 10:45), the believer may plead before the throne of grace the promise of Jesus: "If ye then, being evil, know how to give good gifts unto your children: how much more shall your heavenly Father give the Holy Spirit to them that ask him?" (Luke 11:13).

A certain school of thought teaches that one should not ask for the Spirit for the following reason. At Pentecost the Holy Spirit came to dwell permanently in the Church; since then, every one who is added to the Church by the Lord, and baptized unto Christ, by that very fact becomes a partaker of the Spirit (1 Corinthians 12:13) —or so it is claimed.

The outpouring of the Holy Spirit on the Day of Pentecost was, indeed, dispensational, as some of these good brethren would especially emphasize; and the Holy Spirit is, indeed, present everywhere in the world and distinctively active as the great Administrator in the Church, but His universal presence and availability does not preclude the necessity of individual active appropriation of that presence to bring to the individual an experience distinctly promised— "The promise is unto you, and to your children, and to *all that are afar off,* even *as many as the Lord our God shall call"* (Acts 2:39) —and frequently demonstrated after the Day of Pentecost. Compare Acts 8: 12-17; 10:44-48; 19:1-6.

The work of Christ, while prophetically foretold, was dispensationally completed at Calvary, and that redemptive work, while universally available, yet must be individually appropriated to be efficacious. So is it with the baptism in the Holy Spirit.

Those who emphasize the dispensational aspect of the descent of the Holy Spirit on the Day of Pentecost and affirm that by that coming all who believe in Christ are baptized in the Holy Spirit upon being regenerated, quote 1 Corinthians 12:13 as a proof text for their point—"For by [Greek *in*] one Spirit are we all baptized into one body." But they fail to note that Paul's emphasis here is not upon individual experience, for he is stressing the induction into one body of all classes, Jew, Gentile, bond, free. In fact, 1 Corinthians 12:13 does not refer to the baptism of the Spirit at all, but, in our judgment, to the experience of regeneration by which we are brought into the body of Christ.

It is true that by the ministry of the Holy Spirit we are immersed into or constituted one body in

Christ, but the norm of individual experience of being
"filled with the Spirit" is still to be found in Acts
2:4, 38, 39; 10:44-48; 19:1-5; 8:12-17.

It is true that the Spirit abides in the church, yet
that should not deter the believer from asking and
seeking. As Dr. A. J. Gordon has pointed out, though
the Spirit was given once and for all to the church
on the Day of Pentecost, it does not follow that every
believer has received the Baptism. God's gift requires
an appropriation. God gave (John 3:16) ; we must receive (John 1:12). As sinners we accept Christ; as
saints we accept the Holy Spirit. As there is a faith
toward Christ for salvation, so there is a faith toward
the Spirit for power and consecration.

Pentecost is once for all; the baptism of believers is ever
for all. The shutting up of certain great blessings of the
Holy Ghost within the ideal realm called the "Apostolic
Age," however convenient it may be as an escape from
fancied difficulties, may be the means of robbing believers
of some of their most precious covenant rights.

(f) It may result from individual prayer. Saul of
Tarsus fasted and prayed three days previous to his
being filled with the Holy Spirit (Acts 9:9-17).

(g) It follows obedience. The Holy Ghost is He
"whom God hath given to them that obey him" (Acts
5:32).

(h) Faith also plays its part. If the truth is really
apprehended by a seeker that the baptism in the
Spirit according to the New Testament pattern is *for*

him, he will be expecting the sign of "speaking with tongues." Rightly so. But often there is a temptation to strain, to storm heaven, so to speak, in order to get "through" to an experience as if the Baptizer (our Lord Jesus Christ) were reluctant to bestow it. The procedure, growing out of this misguided attitude of heart and mind, may degenerate into a mere repetition of phrases in seeking the Lord.

All of this leaves out a most essential element in the reception of the baptism—FAITH. Remember that "without faith it is impossible to please him" (Hebrews 11:6). The baptism or any other bestowment from God is on the basis of His promise (cf. Luke 11:13) and must be received by faith. "Whatsoever ye desire, when ye pray, believe ye receive [*have received—* literally] them and ye shall have them" (Mark 11:24).

So the seeker should "believe God" and then, as the evidence of that faith—

(i) There will be praise. Praise, real praise from the depths of the soul, is one of the evidences that faith is active and appropriating. The relation between faith and praise, or thanksgiving, is expressed by the Psalmist: "Then believed they his words, they sang his praise" (Psalm 106:12). Since Christ is the Saviour, thanksgiving should well up in the heart for His "so great salvation," and praiseful expectation from Him, as the Baptizer, should be evident.

Others who may be praying with a seeker may be

helpful in maintaining an environment of faith and praise while he is tarrying.

f. *Glorification*

Will the Holy Spirit be with the believer in heaven or will the Spirit leave him? The answer is that the Holy Spirit in the believer is as a well of living water springing up into *everlasting life* (John 4:14). The indwelling of the Spirit represents just the beginning of life eternal, which will be consummated in the life to come. "Now is our salvation nearer than when we believed," wrote Paul, which words imply that we have only the beginning of a salvation which is to be consummated in the life to come. The Holy Spirit represents the beginning or first part of this complete salvation. This truth is expressed under three illustrations:

(1) *Commercial.* The Spirit is described as "the earnest of our inheritance until the redemption of the purchased possession" (Ephesians 1:14; 2 Corinthians 5:5). The Holy Spirit is a pledge that our deliverance shall be complete. It is more than a pledge; it is an installment handed over in advance as a guarantee that the remainder will follow.

(2) *Agricultural.* The Holy Spirit is the firstfruits of the future life (Romans 8:23). When the Israelite brought the firstfruits of his produce to God's temple, it was an acknowledgment that all belonged to God. The offering of a part symbolized the offering of all. The Holy Spirit in believers is the firstfruits of the glorious harvest to come.

(3) *Domestic.* Just as children are given a slight taste of some delicacy previous to a banquet, so in the experience of the Spirit. Christians have but "tasted . . . the powers of the world to come" (Hebrews 6:5). In Revelation 7:17 we read that "the Lamb which is in the midst of the throne shall . . . lead them unto living fountains of waters." Notice the plural in these last words. In the life to come Christ will be the Giver of the Spirit, and He who imparted the foretaste will lead His followers to fresh supplies of the Spirit and to means of grace and spiritual enrichment unknown during their earthly pilgrimage.

g. *Sins Against the Spirit*

The gracious operations of the Spirit bring great blessings but these involve corresponding responsibilities. Generally speaking, the believers may grieve, lie to the Person of the Spirit, and quench His power (Ephesians 4:30; Acts 5:3, 4; 1 Thessalonians 5:19). Unbelievers may blaspheme the Person of the Spirit and resist His power (Acts 7:51; Matthew 12:31, 32). The context in each case will explain the nature of the sin. William Evans points out: "Resisting has to do with the regenerating work of the Spirit; grieving has to do with the indwelling Holy Spirit; quenching has to do with the enduement for service."

Lesson 10

THE GIFTS OF THE HOLY SPIRIT

a. *The General Nature of the Gifts*

The *gifts* of the Spirit must be distinguished from the *gift* of the Spirit. The former describes the supernatural abilities imparted by the *Spirit* for special ministries; the latter refers to the impartation of the Spirit to believers as ministered by the ascended *Christ* (Acts 2:33).

Paul speaks of the gifts of the Spirit ("spirituals" in the original Greek) in a threefold aspect. They are "charismata," or a variety of gifts bestowed by the one Spirit (1 Corinthians 12:4, 7); "diakonai," or varieties of service rendered in the cause of the one Lord; and "energemata" or varieties of the power of the one God who works all in all. All these aspects are referred to as "the manifestation of the Spirit," which is given to men for the profit of all.

What is the main purpose of the gifts of the Spirit? They are spiritual enablements for the purpose of building up the Church of God through the instruction of believers and the winning of converts (Ephesians 4:7-13). Paul enumerates nine of these gifts in 1 Corinthians 12:8-10, which may be classified as follows:

(1) Those that impart power to *know* supernaturally: the word of wisdom, the word of knowledge, discernment of spirits.

(2) Those that impart power to *act* supernaturally: faith, miracles, healings.

(3) Those that impart power to *speak* supernaturally: prophecy, tongues, interpretation.

These gifts are described as "the manifestation of the Spirit," which is "given to every man to profit withal" (that is, for the benefit of the Church). Here we have the scriptural definition of a "manifestation" of the Spirit—namely, the operation of any of the nine gifts of the Spirit.

b. *The Variety of the Gifts*

(1) *The Word of Wisdom.* By this expression is meant the utterance of wisdom. What kind of wisdom? This will be best determined by noting in what senses the word "wisdom" is used in the New Testament. It is applied to the art of interpreting dreams and giving sage advice (Acts 7:10); the intelligence evinced in discovering the meaning of some mysteri-

ous number or vision (Revelation 13:18; 17:9); skill
in the management of affairs (Acts 6:3); a devout pru-
dence in dealings with those outside the Church (Colossians 4:5); skill and discretion in imparting Christian truth (Colossians 1:28); the knowledge and practice of the requisites for godly and upright living
(James 1:5; 3:13, 17); the knowledge and skill in affairs requisite for the successful defense of Christ's
cause (Luke 21:15); an acquaintance of divine things
and human duties, joined to a power of discoursing
concerning them and of interpreting and applying
sacred Scripture (Matthew 13:54; Mark 6:2; Acts 6:10);
the wisdom and instruction with which John the Baptist and Jesus taught men the plan of salvation (Matthew 11:19). In Paul's writings "wisdom" is applied to:
a knowledge of the divine plan previously hidden,
of providing men with salvation through the atonement of Christ (1 Corinthians 1:30; Colossians 2:3);
hence all the treasures of wisdom are said to be hidden in Christ (Colossians 2:3); the wisdom of God as
evinced in forming and executing His counsels (Romans 11:33).

The word of wisdom, then, would seem to signify
supernatural ability to utter forth wisdom along the
above-mentioned lines.

(2) *The Word of Knowledge* is a supernaturally
inspired utterance of facts. Along what lines? A study
of the New Testament usage of the word "knowledge"
will supply the answer. The word denotes: the knowledge of God, such as is offered in the Gospels (2 Co-

rinthians 2:14), especially in Paul's exposition of it
(2 Corinthians 10:5); the knowledge of the things that
belong to God (Romans 11:33); intelligence and understanding (Ephesians 3:19); the knowledge of the
Christian faith (Romans 15:14; 1 Corinthians 1:5); the
deeper, the more perfect, and enlarged knowledge of
this religion, such as belongs to the more advanced
(1 Corinthians 12:8; 13:2, 8; 14:6; 2 Corinthians 6:6;
8:7; 11:6); the higher knowledge of Christian and
divine things which false teachers boast of (1 Timothy
6:20); moral wisdom such as is seen in right living
(2 Peter 1:5) and in relations with others (1 Peter 3:7);
knowledge concerning things divine and human duties
(Romans 2:20; Colossians 2:3).

What is the difference between wisdom and knowledge? According to one scholar, knowledge is the
insight into divine things, and wisdom is the skill
which regulates the Christian life according to its
foundation principles. Thayer's Lexicon states that
where "knowledge" and "wisdom" are used together,
the former seems to be knowledge regarded by itself;
the latter, knowledge as exhibited in action.

The word of knowledge, then, would seem to be
supernatural ability to express "certain facts in the
mind of God—a fragment of the totality of divine
knowledge" (Horton); or a "revelation of divine truth
operating through the intellectual faculties of the
Spirit-filled believer" (Gee).

(3) *Faith* (Weymouth renders it "special faith").
This must be distinguished from saving faith, and that

confidence in God without which it is impossible to please Him (Hebrews 11:6). It is true that saving faith is described as a gift (Ephesians 2:8), but in this passage "gift" is used as opposed to "works," while in 1 Corinthians 12:9 the word used means a special endowment of the power of the Spirit. What is the gift of faith? Donald Gee describes it as follows:

...a quality of faith, sometimes called by our older theologians the "Faith of Miracles." It would seem to come upon certain of God's servants in times of special crisis or opportunity in such mighty power that they are lifted right out of the realm of even natural and ordinary faith in God, and have a divine certainty put within their souls that triumphs over everything.... Possibly the same quality of faith is the thought of our Lord where He says in Mark 11:22, "Have the faith of God" (margin). It was faith of this peculiar quality of which He could say that a grain of it would remove a mountain (Matthew 17:20). A little of that divine faith which is an attribute of the Almighty, dropped into the soul of man—what miracles it can produce!

Examples of the operation of the gift: 1 Kings 18: 33-35; Acts 3:4.

(4) *Gifts of Healings.* To say that a person has the gifts (note the plurals, perhaps referring to a variety of healings) means that he is used of God in supernaturally ministering health to the sick, through prayer. It seems to be a sign-gift, especially valuable to the evangelist for attracting people's attention to the gospel (Acts 8:6, 7; 28:8-10). It is not to be understood that the possessor of this gift (or the person possessed by this gift) has the power to heal *everyone;* allowance must be made for the sovereignty of God

and the sick person's attitude and spiritual condition. Even Christ was limited in His miracle-working ability by the unbelief of the people (Matthew 13:58).

The sick person is not absolutely dependent upon one possessing the gift. All believers in general, and elders of the church in particular, are empowered to pray for the sick (Mark 16:18; James 5:14).

(5) *The Working of Miracles,* literally, "works of power." The keynote is *power.* Compare John 14:12; Acts 1:8. The "special" miracles at Ephesus are an illustration of the operation of the gift (Acts 19:11, 12; 5:12-15).

(6) *Prophecy.*

Prophecy, generally speaking, is utterance inspired by the Spirit of God. Biblical prophecy may be by revelation, wherein the prophet proclaims a message previously received through a dream, a vision, or the Word of the Lord. Or it may be ecstatic, inspirational utterance on the spur of the moment. There are many scriptural examples of both forms. Ecstatic, inspirational prophecy may take the form of exaltation and worship of Christ, or exhortatory admonition, or inspirational comfort and encouragement to the saints. —J. R. Flower.

Prophecy is distinguished from ordinary preaching in that while the latter is generally the product of the study of existing revelation, prophecy is the result of a spontaneous spiritual inspiration. It was not intended to supplant preaching or teaching but to supplement it with the inspirational touch.

The possession of the gift constituted a person a "prophet." See Acts 15:32; 21:9, 10; 1 Corinthians 14:

29: The purpose of the New Testament gift of prophecy is stated in 1 Corinthians 14:3—the prophet edi-
fies, exhorts, and comforts believers.

The inspiration manifest in the gift of prophecy is
not on a level with that of Scripture. This is implied
by the fact that believers are instructed to test or
judge prophetic messages. See 1 Corinthians 14:29.
Why judge them or test them? For one reason,
because of the possibility of the human spirit (Jeremiah 23:16; Ezekiel 13:2, 3) mingling its message with
that of the divine. 1 Thessalonians 5:19, 22 deals
with the operation of the gift of prophecy. The con-
servative Thessalonians had gone so far in their dis-
trust of these messages (verse 20) that they were in
danger of quenching the Spirit (verse 19); but Paul
tells them to test each message (verse 21), hold on
to what is good (verse 21), and reject what appears
to be unsound (verse 22).

Should prophecy or interpretation be given in the
first person; for example, "It is I, the Lord, who am
speaking to you, My people"? The question is an important one, for the quality of certain messages has
caused people to wonder as to whether the Lord Himself could have spoken thus. The answer may depend
on our view of the mode of inspiration.

Is it *mechanical;* that is, does God use the speaker
as we would use a megaphone, the person being en-
tirely passive and becoming simply a mouthpiece?
Or, is the method *dynamical;* that is, does God supernaturally quicken the spiritual nature (note 1 Co-

rinthians 14:14—"My spirit prayeth") enabling the person to speak the divine message in terms beyond the natural scope of the mental faculties?

If and when God inspires according to the first-named method, the first person would naturally be used. According to the second method the message would be given in the third person; for example, "The Lord would have His people look up and be encouraged," etc.

Many experienced workers believe that interpretation and prophetic messages should be given in the third person. In the only two New Testament instances where prophecy is demonstrated and the actual words given, they are in the third person. See Luke 1:41-45, 67-79.

(7) *Discerning of Spirits.* We have seen that there can exist a false inspiration, the work of seducing spirits or of the human spirit. How shall people detect the difference? By the gift of discernment which enables the possessor to determine whether or not a prophet is speaking by the Spirit of God. This gift enables the possessor to "see through" all outward appearances and know the true nature of an inspiration. The gift of discernment may be checked by two other tests: the doctrinal (1 John 4:1-6) and the practical (Matthew 7:15-23).

For some illustrations of the working of this gift see John 1:47-50; John 3:1-3; John 2:25; 2 Kings 5:20-26; Acts 5:3; 8:23; 16:16-18. These references imply that the gift enables one to discern a person's spiritual character. Distinguish this gift from natural insight into human nature, and above all, from a fault-finding spirit.

(8) *Tongues.* "Divers kinds of tongues."

"The gift of tongues is the power of speaking supernaturally in a language never learned by the speaker, that language being made intelligible to the listeners by means of the equally supernatural gift of interpretation." There seem to be two kinds of messages in tongues: first, ecstatic praise addressed to God alone (1 Corinthians 14:2); and second, a definite message for the church (1 Corinthians 14:5). Distinguish between tongues as a *Sign* and tongues as a *Gift.* The former is for all (Acts 2:4); the latter is not for all (1 Corinthians 12:30).

(9) *Interpretation of Tongues.* Writes Donald Gee:

The purpose of the gift of interpretation is to render the ecstatic and inspired utterances by the Spirit, which have gone forth in a tongue unknown to the vast majority present, available to the general understanding of all, by repeating them distinctly in the ordinary language of the people assembled.

It is purely a spiritual operation. The same Holy Spirit who inspired the speaking in other tongues, whereby the words expressed flow from the spirit rather than through the intellect, is able to inspire the interpretation also. Interpretation is therefore inspirational, ecstatic, spontaneous. As the utterance, when speaking in tongues, is not conceived in the mind, so the utterance of interpretation emanates from the spirit rather than from the intellect of man.

Notice that tongues plus interpretation are equal to prophecy. (See 1 Corinthians 14:5.) Why not then be content with prophecy? Because tongues are a "sign" for the unbeliever (1 Corinthians 14:22).

Note. It has been suggested that the ministries enumerated in Romans 12:6-8 and 1 Corinthians 12:28 should also be included under the classification of "charismata"—thus broadening the scope of spiritual gifts to include all Spirit-inspired ministrations.

c. *The Charismata of Romans* 12:4-8

It is striking to note that the Spirit through Paul takes the "gift" of prophecy from among the "nine" of 1 Corinthians 12 to introduce and to form a connecting link between this former group of "charismata" and the latter group in Romans 12, and to indicate that the latter group are in the same category of gracious enablements of the Holy Spirit as the former. This is proved also by Paul's statement in 1 Corinthians 12:28, where prophecy, teaching, helps (ministration), governments (rule), found in Romans 12, are mentioned.

Prophecy has already been discussed but we shall further refer to it in relation to its context here in Romans. After giving that earnest appeal to the believer ("I beseech") for the consecration of his whole being to the will of God (verse 1), Paul sounds a warning note against an undue self-estimate, and a corresponding exhortation to estimate one's self with discrimination and sober judgment (verse 3). Paul has a standard by which self-estimate is to be regulated, expressed by "according as." Further, this scale or measurement is different in different persons, expressed in the statement, "as God hath dealt [imparted or distributed] to each man a measure of faith." "The character of this measure or standard is determined by faith," says Dr. Marvin Vincent in his *Word Studies in the New Testament,* and he further says "it must be observed that the general exhortation to a proper self-estimate is shaped by, and foreshadows, the subsequent words respecting differences of gifts (charismata). It was at this point that the tendency to self-conceit and spiritual arrogance would develop itself." Dr. Vincent further comments: "Sound and correct views as to the character and extent of spiritual gifts and functions are fixed by a measure, the determining element of which, in each particular case, is faith."

Paul's meaning in this whole context is illustrated by the symbolism of the body (verses 4, 5), made up of members differing in function and prominence. He expresses the thought that spiritual "gifts," whatever their nature, are to be exercised in recognition of mutual dependence of each member of the body upon the other, and that each "charisma" be exercised in faith within the limits God has prescribed to each believer, without ambition to assume any other member's place or to exercise authority not bestowed upon him.

(1) *Ministry*. This word, from the Greek "diakonia,"
is a broad word and appears always in the New Testament in connection with the service in the Christian
Church, with these three exceptions: Martha's serving
(Luke 10:40); the ministry of angels (Hebrews 1:14);
and the ministry of Moses (2 Corinthians 3:7). It is
difficult to fix its precise meaning here, but it is used
of service in general, including all forms of Christian
ministration tending to the good of the Christian body
(1 Corinthians 12:5; Ephesians 4:12; 2 Timothy 4:11);
of the apostolic office and its administration in general (Acts 20:24; 2 Corinthians 4:1; 1 Timothy 1:12);
or of that office defined as a ministry of reconciliation,
of the Word, of the Spirit, and of righteousness (2 Corinthians 5:18; Acts 6:4; 2 Corinthians 3:8, 9).

It is distinguished from prophecy, exhortation, and
teaching in this passage, and almost any other work
may be included in it.

So the Lord has graced certain individuals who are
ready and willing to fit in anywhere with a joyous
spirit of service in behalf of the body of Christ. The
words in verse 7, "Let us wait on" (or, as in the
revised version, "Let us give ourselves to") are necessary to the sense and imply the wholehearted consecration of the individual to whatever service—whether public, or hidden and more obscure.

(2) *Teaching*. The ministry of the teacher, as one
of those personal gifts which Christ has bestowed upon His Church, is a very important one and frought

both with great possibilities of blessing, guidance, and instruction, and on the other hand with great danger to the Church. Someone has said that it is the teachers that have been responsible for so many of the schisms in the Church. By this of course was not meant those who occupied a place in the classroom, but those leaders whose work it was to lay foundational interpretations of Scripture. Great church leaders like Luther and Zwingli were also teachers, and their difference over the interpretation of Christ's words, "This is my body"—whether literal or figurative—split the Reformation in two.

May the Lord guide and keep very humble the teacher, whose office is often combined with that of pastor. His office has not always been appreciated, for his appeal is to the intellectual faculties in making truth clear through logical processes. But this ministry is none the less vital, for truth has to be understood first before it can make its impact upon the emotions of the soul, and be accepted intelligently by the will.

Believers who are constantly coming into "the faith" through the ministry of the evangelist need to be indoctrinated in the principles of the faith and guided in their walk. Surely to fulfill this ministry there must needs be a "charisma," a gracious enabling of God.

(3) *Exhortation.* "Exhortation is such a distinct phase of the gift of prophecy (see 1 Corinthians 14:3) that it is dignified by being called a 'gift' (charisma)

itself. Here is the emotional appeal characteristic of
the gifts of utterance—not just an emotional outburst
by way of relief for pent-up feelings, but a controlled
stream of earnest, vibrant Holy Spirit words directed
to sinner or saint with a plea to turn from wrong to
right, from error to truth, to obedience and faith. God
loves and God pleads (by means of exhortation exercised) through the 'gift' of prophecy."—*Riggs*.

(4) *Christian Benevolence*. The apostle Paul, in his
second letter to the Corinthians, distinctly refers in
those classic chapters on Christian benevolence to this
practical manifestation of essential love and unselfish-
ness as a "grace" (charis). See 2 Corinthians 8:6, 7.

One who has opened his heart so completely in
personal consecration as to be "graced" of God in this
ministry, occupies a large and important place indeed
in the divine economy. The writer had a godly Christian uncle, a wealthy businessman, who began his
business career with a plan to lay aside a tenth of
the firm's income (a separate set of books was kept
for this) for Christian benevolence—foreign missions,
etc. This "grace" so increased in and upon him that
he increased his giving to two-tenths, three-tenths,
and for years before his death he administered everything above his living expenses to effective Christian
giving.

Here is a "gift" that everyone of God's children
can receive and express "with simplicity" (liberality)
for the glory of God and for the extension of His
kingdom.

(5) *Administration*. In the economy of God's church there must of necessity be those who occupy positions of leadership, with the responsibility of guiding and directing the activities of the church locally and more widely. The word "ruleth" (verse 8) is from a Greek word which means "the one standing in front." The same word is used in 1 Thessalonians 5:12, where it is translated "are over you"—literally, "those who stand in front of you," your leaders in the Lord, presbyters, bishops (literally, "overseers"), and deacons.

Such men have great responsibility and are exhorted in Romans 12:8 "to rule with diligence" (literally, "haste," or "dispatch"—that is, earnestly, as realizing the dignity and responsibility with which God has "graced" them, and the urgency of the eternal issues at stake).

The exhortation to the church at Thessalonica was that the church should get acquainted with their leaders and follow them. Theirs is a thankless but necessary task, and often involves what Paul indicates in the literal language of "admonish" in 1 Thessalonians 5:12, which is a translation of an old verb meaning "putting sense into the heads of people."—From *Word Pictures in the New Testament*, by Dr. A. T. Robertson.

Surely this is a phase of the church's equipment requiring that such rulers be "graced" of God.

(6) *Showing Mercy*. One bestowment of God which we all must have received as sinners was "mercy,"

and the child of God continues to need mercy from God in all his approach to Him. We are exhorted to come "boldly [literally, 'with a fearlessly outspoken plea'] to the throne of grace, that we may obtain mercy, and find grace to help in time of need" (Hebrews 4:16).

How necessary, then, that God's church, in turn, should be widely "graced" with those who show mercy out of sympathetic, understanding hearts, accompanied by cheerfulness (literally, "with joyous hilarity"); that is, that the opportunities to show mercy be embraced with joy and that its exercise bring joy to others.

Lesson 11

THE GIFTS OF THE HOLY SPIRIT (Continued)

d. *Regulating the Gifts.*

The lightning that rends trees, burns houses, and destroys people is of the same nature as the electricity that operates so smoothly through a power house. The difference lies in the matter of control. In 1 Corinthians 12 Paul has revealed the mighty spiritual resources of power available for the church; in the fourteenth chapter he exhibits the "controls" by which this power is to be regulated, so that it will build up rather than destroy the church. The instruction was needed, for a reading of this chapter will show that pandemonium had been reigning in some meetings due to a lack of knowledge of spiritual manifestations. Chapter fourteen lays down the following principles for such regulation:

(1) *Proportionate Value.* Verses 5-19. The Corinthians had become overbalanced on the gift of tongues,

no doubt because of its spectacular nature; but Paul reminds them that interpretation and prophecy are needed so that the people might have an intelligent knowledge of what is being said.

(2) *Edification.* The purpose of the gifts is the building up of the Church, by encouraging believers and converting the unsaved. But, says Paul, if an outsider enters the church and hears nothing but uninterpreted speaking in tongues, he will rightly conclude that the people are demented. Verses 12, 23.

(3) *Wisdom.* Verse 20. "Brethren, be not children in understanding." In other words, "Use your common sense."

(4) *Self-control.* Verse 32. Some Corinthians might protest: We cannot be silent: if God's Spirit comes upon us, we just *have* to speak out. Answers Paul, "The spirits of the prophets are subject to the prophets." That is, the one possessing the gift of tongues can control his utterance and speak to God alone, when such control is advisable.

(5) *Orderliness.* Verse 40. "Let all things be done decently and in order." The Holy Spirit, the great Designer of all the beauty of the universe, will certainly not inspire that which is disorderly, or disgraceful. When the Holy Spirit is working in power there will be a stirring and a moving, and those who have learned how to yield to Him will not create unedifying scenes.

(6) *Teachableness.* One may infer from verses 36,

37 that some of the Corinthians had resented the criticism of some of their leaders.

Note 1. The fourteenth chapter of 1 Corinthians implies that there exists power to be controlled. Therefore the chapter would be meaningless to a church which does not experience the manifestations of the Spirit. It is quite true that the Corinthians had gotten off the track in the matter of spiritual gifts—but they had a track to be thrown off from! Had Paul acted like certain modern critics, he would have taken the track away; instead, he wisely put them back on the track.

When the church of the second and third centuries reacted against some extravagances, they went to the opposite extreme and left very little place for the Spirit's operations. But that is only part of the explanation for the cooling off of the church's enthusiasm and the general cessation of spiritual manifestations. Early in the history of the Church there began a process if centralizing of organization and the formulating of hard and fast creeds. While all this was necessary as a defense against false cults, it tended to check the free moving of the Spirit and make Christianity a matter of orthodoxy rather than of spiritual vitality.

Writes Dr. W. T. Rees:

In the first century, the Spirit was known by His manifestations, but in the second century and afterwards, by the rule of the church, and any spiritual phenomenon that did not conform to that rule was attributed to evil spirits.

The same causes have, in modern times, resulted in a neglect of the doctrine and work of the Holy Spirit, a neglect recognized and deplored by many religious leaders.

Nevertheless, the flow of the Spirit has never failed to burst through all hindrances of indifference and formalism, and work in revival power.

Note 2. One should differentiate between *manifestations* and *reactions*. To illustrate: the light in the electric bulb is a *manifestation* of electricity; it is the nature of electricity to manifest itself as light. But when a person touches a live wire and lets out an ear-splitting scream, we cannot describe that scream as a manifestation of electricity; for it is not in the nature of electricity to manifest itself in a spoken voice. What occurred was the person's *reaction* to the electrical power. Naturally the reaction will be conditioned by the person's character and temperament. Some well-controlled individuals might simply gasp and say nothing.

Let us apply this rule to spiritual power. The operations of the gifts in 1 Corinthians 12:7-10 are scripturally described as manifestations of the Spirit. But many actions commonly called "manifestations" are really people's *reactions* to the moving of the Spirit. This refers to such actions as shouting, weeping, raising the hands and others.

What practical value is there in the knowledge of this distinction? (a) It will enable us to honor and recognize the working of the Spirit without charging up to Him everything that may be done at a meeting. Critics, ignoring the distincton referred to, incorrectly conclude that because an individual's actions may not be elegant or "esthetic," such a person is not under the inspiration of the Spirit. Such critics may be likened to a person who, seeing the antics of an electrically shocked person, exclaims in disgust, "Electricity simply does not act that way!" The direct impact of the Holy Spirit is of so stirring a nature that frail human flesh may well be excused for not acting as calmly and indifferently as it would under the moving of a gentle breeze. (b) The knowledge of the distinction will naturally encourage one to react to the moving of the Spirit in a manner that will always glorify God. Certainly it would be just as unfair to criticize a young convert's extravagances as to criticize the stumblings and falls of a babe learning to walk. But at the same time, judging from 1 Corinthians 14, it is clear that God wants His people to react to the Spirit in an intelligent, edifying, and self-disciplined manner. "Seek that ye may excel to the edifying of the church" (14:12).

e. *Receiving the Gifts*

God is sovereign in the matter of the bestowal of gifts; he is the One to decide what kind of gift shall be imparted. He may impart a gift without human intervention at all, and even without the person's asking. But generally God works in cooperation with man, and there is something that man can do about the matter. What is required of those who would have the gifts?

(1) *Submission to the Will of God.* Not what *I* want, but what He wants, should be the attitude. We may want some spectacular gift; He may decide otherwise.

(2) *Holy Ambition.* "Desire spiritual gifts" (1 Corinthians 12:31; 14:1). Ambition has been often directed toward wrong and harmful ends, but that is no reason why we should not consecrate it to the service of God.

(3) *Strong desire* for gifts will naturally result in prayer, but always in submission to God. Compare 1 Kings 3:5-10; 2 Kings 2:9, 10.

(4) *Faith.* "Should we *tarry* for the gifts?" some have asked. Since spiritual gifts are "tools" for the upbuilding of the church, it seems more reasonable to go right to work for God and then trust Him to impart the gift necessary for the particular task. Thus

the Sunday school teacher will trust God for the operation of the gifts necessary for a teacher; so will the pastor, the evangelist, and the lay member. A good way to secure a position is to go prepared to work; a good way to receive spiritual gifts is to be "on the job" for God, instead of sitting down with folded hands and waiting for gifts to drop from heaven.

(5) *Yieldedness.* The fire of inspiration may be quenched (1 Thessalonians 5:19) through negligence; hence the need of stirring up (literally, "kindling") the gift that is in us (2 Timothy 1:6; 1 Timothy 4:14).

f. *Testing the Gifts*

The Scriptures admit the possibility of demonic inspiration, as well as of supposedly prophetic messages originating in one's spirit. The following tests are laid down whereby one may distinguish the true inspiration from the false.

(1) *Loyalty to Christ.* While in Ephesus, Paul received a letter from the Corinthian church containing certain inquiries, one of which was "concerning spiritual gifts." 1 Corinthians 12:3 suggests a probable reason for the inquiry. During one of their meetings, when the gift of prophecy was in operation, a voice was heard crying out, "Jesus is accursed!" It is possible that some heathen soothsayer or temple devotee had attended their meeting and when the power fell upon the Christians these pagans yielded to demonic control and opposed the confession, "Jesus is Lord,"

with the diabolic denial, "Jesus is accursed!" The records of modern missions in China and other countries could supply similar instances.

Paul immediately explains to the perplexed and distressed Corinthians that there are two kinds of inspiration, divine and demonic, and explains the difference. He reminds them of the demonic impulses and ecstasies they had experienced or witnessed in some idol temples, and points out that this inspiration led to idol worship. See 1 Corinthians 10:20. On the other hand, the Spirit of God inspires people to confess the Lordship of Jesus. "Wherefore I give you to understand, that no man speaking by the Spirit of God calleth Jesus accursed: and that no man can say that Jesus is the Lord, but by the Holy Ghost." Compare Revelation 19:10; Matthew 16:16, 17; 1 John 4:1, 2.

Of course, this does not mean that a person cannot say in parrotlike fashion that Jesus is Lord. The meaning is that no one can utter the *heart conviction* of the deity of Jesus without the illumination of the Holy Spirit. Compare Romans 10:9.

(2) *The Practical Test.* The Corinthians were spiritual in the sense that they displayed a keen interest in spiritual gifts (1 Corinthians 12:1; 14:12). But while glorying in the Spirit's energizing power they seemed lacking in His sanctifying power. They were fostering factions; the church was tolerating a case of unspeakable immorality; brethren were going to law with one another; some were slipping back to

pagan standards; others had partaken of the Lord's Supper in a drunken condition.

We may be sure that the apostle did not judge these converts too harshly, for he remembered the vile pit of heathenism from which they had been recently rescued and the temptations with which they were surrounded. But he felt that they must be impressed with the truth that, however important spiritual gifts might be, Christian character and right living must be the supreme aim of their endeavors. After encouraging them to "covet earnestly the best gifts" (1 Corinthians 12:31), he adds, "and yet shew I unto you a more excellent way." Then follows his sublime discourse on divine love, the crown of character.

But right here we must be careful to distinguish between things that differ. Opponents of speaking in tongues (who, by the way, are unscriptural in their attitude, 1 Corinthians 14:39), maintain that people would do better to seek love which is the supreme gift. They are guilty of confused thinking. Love is not a gift but a fruit of the Spirit. The fruit of the Spirit is the progressive development of the Christ-life implanted at regeneration; while the gifts may be bestowed suddenly to any Spirit-filled believer at any point in the believer's experience. The first represents the sanctifying power of the Spirit, while the second involves His energizing power.

Nevertheless, one will make no mistake in insisting upon the supremacy of Christian character. Perplexing as it may appear, it is a fact of experience that persons defective in holiness may exhibit manifestations of the gifts. But the following facts should be pondered: (a) The baptism in the Holy Spirit does not make a person immediately perfect. Enduement of power is one thing; maturity of Christian graces is another. Both the new birth and the baptism with the Holy Spirit are gifts of God's grace and reveal His grace toward us. There may still remain a need for a personal sanctification which comes through an operation of the Holy Spirit, developing the grace of God within us. (b) The operation of the gifts does not have a sanctifying power. Balaam experienced the gift of prophecy while in the depths of his heart he wanted to betray God's people for money. (c) Paul tells us plainly of the possibility of possessing the gifts without possessing love.

Serious consequences may ensue for the one who exercises the gifts apart from love. First, he will be a constant stumblingblock to those who know his real character; second, the gifts profit him nothing. No amount of spiritual manifestations, no zeal in the ministry, no accomplishing of results, can make up for lack of personal holiness (Hebrews 12:14).

(3) *The Doctrinal Test.* The Holy Spirit has come to operate in the sphere of truth relating to Christ's deity and atoning work. It is unthinkable that He should contradict what had already been revealed by Christ to His apostles. Therefore, for example, any prophet who denies the incarnation of Christ cannot be speaking by the Spirit of God (1 John 4:2, 3).

Lesson 12

THE HOLY SPIRIT IN THE CHURCH

a. *The Advent of the Holy Spirit*

The Saviour lived before His incarnation and continued to live after His ascension; but during the intervening period He exercised what we may call His dispensational or "temperal" mission which He came into the world to fulfill; and having accomplished it, He returned to the Father. So the Spirit came into the world at an appointed time for a definite mission and will leave when His mission is accomplished. He came to earth not only for an appointed purpose but also for an appointed time.

There are three major dispensations in the Scriptures corresponding to the Three Persons of the Godhead. The Old Testament is the dispensation of the Father; Christ's earthly ministry is the dispensation of the Son; and the age between the ascension and the second coming of Christ is the dispensation of the

Spirit. The Spirit's ministry will continue until Jesus comes, after which another dispensational ministry will succeed. The characteristic name for the Spirit during this dispensation is the Spirit of Christ.

The entire Trinity cooperates in the full manifestation of God during the great dispensations. Each exercises an earthly ministry: the Father descends at Sinai, the Son descends at the Incarnation, the Spirit descends on the Day of Pentecost. The Father commends the Son from heaven (Matthew 3:17), the Son commends the Spirit (Revelation 2:11), and the Spirit testifies to the Son (John 15:26). As God the Son fulfills to men the work of God the Father, so the Holy Ghost fulfills to men the work of God the Son.

John Owen, a theologian of the seventeenth century, points out how, throughout the dispensations, there are certain tests of orthodoxy related to each of the three Persons. Before the advent of Christ the great test was the oneness of God, Creator and Ruler of all. After the coming of Christ the great question was whether a church orthodox on the first point would now receive the Divine Son, incarnate, sacrificed, risen and ascended, according to the promise. And when the working of this test had gathered out the church of Christian believers, the Holy Spirit came into prominence as the touchstone of true faith. "The sin of despising His Person and rejecting His work now is of the same nature with the idolatry of old, and with the Jews' rejection of the Person of the Son."

As the eternal Son became incarnate in a human

body at His birth, so the eternal Spirit became incarnate in the Church which is His body. This occurred on the Day of Pentecost, "the birthday of the Spirit" in His dispensational ministry to the Church. What the cradle was to the incarnate Christ, the upper room was to the Spirit. Note what occurred on that memorable day.

(1) *The Birth of the Church.* "And when the Day of Pentecost was fully come." Pentecost was an Old Testament feast that occurred fifty days after the Passover, for which reason it is called "Pentecost," which means "fifty." See Leviticus 23:15-21. Let us notice its position in the festal calendar. (a) First came the Passover feast, which commemorated the deliverance of Israel in Egypt in the night when the death angel slew the firstborn of Egypt while God's people ate the lamb in houses sealed with blood. This is typical of the death of Christ, the Lamb of God, whose blood shelters us from the judgment of God. (b) On the Sabbath after the Passover night a sheaf of barley which had already been marked out was reaped by the priests and offered before Jehovah as the firstfruits of the harvest. The principle was that the first part of the harvest must be offered to Jehovah in recognition of His rulership and ownership. After this, the remainder of the harvest could be reaped. This is a type of Christ, "the first-fruits of them that slept" (1 Corinthians 15:20). Christ was the first to be reaped from the field of death and to ascend to the Father never to die again; being the firstfruits, He is the guarantee that all who believe on Him shall follow

Him in the resurrection to life everlasting. (c) Forty-nine days were to be counted from the offering of this wave sheath, and on the fiftieth day—Pentecost —two loaves, the first loaves made from the wheat harvest, were waved before God. Before any loaves could be made and eaten the first two must be offered to Jehovah in acknowledgment of His rulership over the world. After that, other loaves could be baked and eaten. The following is the typical meaning: The hundred and twenty in the upper room were the firstfruits of the Christian church, offered up before the Lord by the Holy Spirit fifty days after the resurrection of Christ. It was the firstborn of the multiplied thousands of churches that have since been established during the last nineteen centuries.

(2) *The Evidence of Christ's Glorification*. The descent of the Holy Spirit was a supernatural "telegram," so to speak, announcing Christ's arrival at the right hand of the Father. See Acts 2:33.

"How do you know that your mother is upstairs?" asked a man of his nephews as they studied their Sunday school lesson.

"I saw her go," answered one.

"You mean that you saw her *start* upstairs," said the uncle. "Perhaps she did not get there, and she may not be there now even if she has been there."

"I know that she is there," replied the youngest child, "for I went to the foot of the steps and called her and she answered me."

The disciples knew that their Master had ascended because He answered them by the "sound from heaven."

(3) *The Completion of Christ's Work.* The Exodus was not complete until fifty days later when at Sinai Israel was organized as the people of God. In like manner the benefit of the atonement was not completed, in the fullest sense, until the Day of Pentecost, when the outpouring of the Spirit was a sign that Christ's sacrifice was accepted in heaven, and that the time had therefore come to proclaim His finished work.

(4) *The Anointing of the Church.* As the Lord's baptism had been followed by His ministry in Galilee, so the baptism of the church was to be preparatory to a worldwide ministry: a ministry not like His own —creative of a new order—but one of simple testimony; yet only to be fulfilled in the power of the Spirit of God.

(5) *The Indwelling of the Church.* After Israel's organization at Sinai, Jehovah came down to dwell in their midst, His presence being localized in the Tabernacle. On the Day of Pentecost the Holy Spirit came down to dwell in the Church as in a temple, His presence being localized in the collective body and individual Christians. The Spirit came into His office to administer the affairs of Christ's kingdom. This fact is recognized throughout the Book of Acts; for example, when Ananias and Sapphira lied to Peter they were really lying to the Holy Ghost who dwelt and ministered in the Church.

(6) *The Beginning of a Dispensation.* The Pentecostal outpouring was not merely a miraculous dis-

play of power intended to arrest attention and invite
inquiry into the new faith. It was the beginning of
a new dispensation. It was an advent of the Spirit
as the Incarnation was the advent of the Son. God
sent forth His Son, and when the mission of the Son
had been fulfilled, He sent forth the Spirit of His Son
to take up the work under new conditions.

b. *The Ministry of the Holy Spirit*

The Holy Spirit is Christ's representative to whom
has been committed the entire administration of the
church until Jesus comes. Christ took His seat in
heaven as "head over all things to the church," and
the Spirit came down to begin the work of building
up the body of Christ. The perfecting of the body of
Christ is the final purpose of the Comforter.

Belief in the Spirit's guidance was deeply rooted
in the Early Church. There was no domain of life
where His right to control was not recognized, and
where the fact of His control was not experienced.
The church committed her whole life to the Spirit's
leading. She continued to reject set forms of worship
until, towards the close of the century, the influence
of the Spirit began to wane and ecclesiasticism took
the place of the Spirit's control.

The Spirit's control is recognized in the following
aspects of the life of the church.

(1) *Administration.* The great missionary move-
ments of the Early Church were commanded and
approved by the Spirit (Acts 8:29; 10:19, 44; 13:2, 4).

Paul was conscious that his whole ministry was inspired by the Holy Ghost (Romans 15:18, 19). On all his journeys he recognized the Spirit's leading (Acts 16:6, 7). The Spirit guided the church in her organization (Acts 6:3; 20:28).

(2) *Preaching.* The first Christians were accustomed to hearing the gospel preached "with the Holy Ghost sent down from heaven" (1 Peter 1:12), which they received "with joy of the Holy Ghost" (1 Thessalonians 1:6). "For our gospel came not unto you in word only, but also in power, and in the Holy Ghost, and in much assurance" (1 Thessalonians 1:5). A. J. Gordon many years ago made the remark: "Our age is losing its grip on the supernatural—the pulpit is descending to the level of the platform."

(3) *Prayer.* Jesus, following John, taught His disciples a model of prayer as a guide for their petitions. But before leaving He spoke of a new kind of prayer, prayer "in my name" (John 16:23), not the repeating of His name as a kind of charm, but the approaching of God spiritually united to Christ by the Spirit. Thus we pray as though we stood with Jesus Himself in God's presence. Paul speaks of "praying always with all prayer and supplication in the Spirit" (Ephesians 6:18); Jude describes true Christians as "praying in the Holy Ghost" (verse 20); and in Romans 8:26, 27 we are told that the Spirit is doing the same thing *in* us that Christ is doing *for* us in heaven— that is, interceding for us (Hebrews 7:25). As Christ on earth taught His disciples how to pray, so today

He teaches the same lesson by means of the Comforter or Helper. Then it was by an outward form; now it is by an inward guidance.

(4) *Singing.* As a result of being filled with the Spirit, believers will be found "speaking to yourselves in psalms and hymns and spiritual songs, singing and making melody in your heart to the Lord" (Ephesians 5:18, 19). "Speaking to yourselves" implies congregational singing. "Psalms" may refer to the Old Testament Psalms, which were sung or chanted; "spiritual songs" denotes spontaneous outburst of melody and praise directly inspired by the Holy Spirit.

(5) *Demonstration.* Many good folk, who are really "on the outside looking in," who have not experienced the joy of the baptism in the Spirit, have been very critical of the exuberance, the freedom, and the outward expressions of emotion which have characterized Pentecostal gatherings, and have cried, "Fanaticism!" It might well be that fanaticism has been present at times among some misguided people, untaught in the Word of God, but there is scriptural ground for many things to which opponents object.

That there is something in the stately processional, the robed choir, the gorgeous priestly vestments, the lighted altar, etc., in the order of liturgical worship found in the great cathedrals of Christendom, that appeals to the esthetic taste of the natural man, no one would deny. But all this outward pomp and glory is purely objective and does not touch the inner springs of the heart. It is beautiful, but cold.

When a soul experiences the joy of sins forgiven, and the further joy of the divine presence, so richly bestowed in the baptism in the Spirit, the emotional nature is moved upon, the "living waters" in the innermost being are agitated and as a result there is of necessity outward expression.

Let us remember that our God is a being of infinite emotion inherent in His very attributes—love, mercy, kindness, anger, etc. This is clearly demonstrated in the life of our Lord Jesus Christ who is the revelation of the Father. Jesus *wept,* His heart was *moved with compassion,* He *groaned in spirit.* Is it strange, then, that we who are made in the image and likeness of God should also partake of the divine emotional nature?

Let us examine the scriptural teaching concerning emotional expression and we shall find that it is clear as regards a number of things that occur in Pentecostal gatherings.

The enemies of the early Friends called them Quakers, because of the bodily agitations that took place in their meetings. Can anyone deny the godliness of George Fox, founder of this group, and of subsequent leaders of this simple people?

The Psalmist exclaimed: "The Lord reigneth, let the people tremble" (Psalm 99:1). It is true that trembling may be the result of fear, but contemplation of the holiness of God and the very nearness of the divine presence in a meeting, may also be the occasion of this manifestation.

(a) *Shouting*. People give vent to their enjoyment of games, and spectacles of various kinds, in the shout. It is most evident that the temple worship of old was often characterized, under the leadership of the musicians and of the "sons of Korah," by the shouting of the people. Compare Psalm 47:1, 5. When the Lord returns, it will be "with a shout..." (1 Thessalonians 4:16). Plenty of demonstration then! If Israel of old shouted and praised God under the law, why not a little shouting in this present glorious dispensation of the grace of God, when the Lord's presence is manifested, and in anticipation of that wondrous return of our Lord?

Israel is prophetically exhorted to "cry out and shout" when their Messiah King is again in their midst during the Millennium (Isaiah 12:6).

(b) *Clapping of Hands*. Psalm 47:1 gives clear exhortation to God's people—"Clap your hands." When Joash was crowned the people "clapped their hands and said, 'God save the king!' " (2 Kings 11:12). Surely the child of God may express his delight from a heart inspired by the Holy Spirit, in contemplation of the crowning day of our Lord Jesus Christ.

(c) *Lifting up of Hands*. Again the Scriptures instruct us: "Lift up your hands in the sanctuary and bless the Lord" (Psalm 134:2). Paul's instruction to the church (1 Timothy 2:8) is in similar vein. This procedure is surely a scriptural way of prayer and worship. When Israel fought against Amalek, there was victory all the while the hands of Moses were up-

raised and supported by Aaron and Hur. The up-
lifted hands today are a sign of victory, of faith and
anticipation, and of outreach of the soul toward God.

(d) *Prostration.* Although not necessarily an accompaniment of the baptism in the Spirit, many times
prostration does occur under the mighty power of
God and the overwhelming sense of His holy presence. Surely if the apostle John, the disciple who
seemed best acquainted with the Lord Jesus, "fell at
his feet as one dead" in His wonderful presence
(Revelation 1:17), is it strange that those who are
less acquainted with Him should fall prostrate too?

Daniel, the "man greatly beloved," to whom the
glorious coming Messiah appeared (Daniel 10:2-6),
was prostrated in His presence (Daniel 10:8, 9).

Should it be considered out of order if, with an
overwhelming sense of one's unworthiness, or with a
heart literally bursting with joy in the manifest presence of the same Lord by the Holy Spirit, the physical
man should be prostrate?

(6) *Testimony.* There did not exist in the primitive
church that line of separation between ministry and
laity observed in Christendom today.

The church was governed by a group or council
of elders but the ministry of public utterance was
not rigidly confined to them. Whoever was endowed
with a gift of the Spirit—whether prophecy, teaching,
knowledge, tongues or interpretation—was permitted
to contribute his portion to the service.

The metaphor "body of Christ" well describes the functioning of collective worship under the control of the Spirit. It brings to our mind a scene of members one after another performing their separate functions in the complete act of worship and all alike controlled by the same animating Power.

c. *The Ascension of the Holy Spirit*

What is true of Christ is true of the Spirit. After accomplishing His dispensational mission He will return to heaven in a body which He has fashioned for Himself—that "new man" (Ephesians 2:15), which is the Church, which is His body. The distinctive work of the Spirit is "to gather out a people for his [Christ's] name" (Acts 15:14), and when this is accomplished and the "fulness of the Gentiles be come in" (Romans 11:25), there will take place the rapture, which, in the words of A. J. Gordon, is "the earthly Christ (1 Corinthians 12:12, 27) rising to meet the heavenly Christ." As Christ shall ultimately give up His kingdom to the Father, so the Holy Ghost shall give up His administration to the Son.

Some have concluded that the Spirit will no longer be in the world after the taking away of the Church. This cannot be correct, for the Holy Spirit, as Deity, is omnipresent. What will take place is the conclusion of the Spirit's dispensational mission as the Spirit of Christ, after which He will still be in the world in another and different relationship.

Ultimately the Lord will "shake not the earth only,

but also heaven" (Hebrews 12:26). When Jehovah manifested His glorious presence upon Sinai when the law was given, even His servant Moses exceedingly feared and quaked (Acts 7:32). True, this was a unique display of God's majesty and power with a specific purpose in view as pertaining to Israel, but God displayed such power when His Spirit was poured out upon the early Christians (Acts 4:31) — "the place was shaken where they were assembled." Would it be any wonder if they who were in the "shaken" place might also themselves have been shaken?

STUDY QUESTIONS—UNIT TWO

LESSON NINE

1. Give some evidence of spiritual manifestations since Pentecost.

2. Show that there was a distinction in the Early Church between those endued with power and those not so endued.

3. Show conclusively that the work of the Holy Spirit is continued after the Baptism.

4. Discuss thoroughly the manner of receiving the Holy Spirit.

5. Refute the argument that everyone is baptized with the Holy Spirit at regeneration.

6. What will be the relation of the Holy Spirit to the believer's glorification?

7. Explain the descriptive terms, "commercial," "agricultural," and "domestic" as relating to the Holy Spirit and the believer.

8. State and explain the sins against the Spirit.

LESSON TEN

1. Discuss the general nature of the gifts of the Spirit.

2. Tell what you can of the word of wisdom.

3. The word of knowledge.

4. Faith.

5. Gifts of healings.

6. Working of miracles.

7. Prophecy.

8. Give reasons for the position that prophecy or interpretation is more fitting in the third person.

9. Describe the gift of discerning of spirits.

10. The gift of tongues.

11. Interpretation of tongues.

12. What is the link Paul uses to connect the nine gifts of 1 Corinthians 12 with the charismata of Romans 12:4-8?

13. Discuss the gift of ministry.

14. Of teaching.

15. Of exhortation.

16. Of a Christian's benevolence.

17. Of administration.

18. Of showing mercy.

LESSON ELEVEN

1. What factors enter into a proper regulation of the gifts of the Spirit?

2. Discuss each factor briefly.

3. What factors relate to the receiving of spiritual gifts?

4. Discuss each briefly.

5. On what three bases may the operation of gifts in the assembly be tested?

6. Discuss each point carefully.

LESSON TWELVE

1. Tell what you can of the Persons of the Trinity as related to the dispensations.

2. In what respects is the Holy Spirit related to the church in His coming at Pentecost?

3. Discuss each point carefully.

4. How is the Holy Spirit related to the church now as to ministry?

6. Explain the scripturalness of various demonstrations of the Holy Spirit in the church.

7. Tell something of the relation of the Spirit to the church in the end of this dispensation.

5. Tell something of His ministry in—

   a. Administration. b. Preaching. c. Prayer.

   d. Singing.

Notes

Notes

Notes